Your First
90 Days
In Network Marketing

Richard Ramos

DOWNLINEUNIVERSITY™

www.DownlineUniversity.com

Your First 90 Days In Network Marketing

Published by
Downline University

Edited by Jacquelynn Ramos

ISBN-13: 978-0615452487
ISBN-10: 0615452485

www.DownlineUniversity.com
www.Richard Ramos.com

Manufactured in the United States of America
10 9 8 7 6 5 4 3 2 1

This book is available at quantity discounts for bulk purchases. For information call: 1-800-220-8457

Your First
90 Days
In Network Marketing

Richard Ramos

Prepare Yourself For Greatness

"The difference between a successful person
and others is not a lack of strength,
not a lack of knowledge,
but rather a lack of will."

Vince Lombardi

Table of Contents

About The Author

Richard Ramos has over 25 years experience in the area of cutting edge technologies including computers and multimedia over the internet, that have led him to develop online marketing strategies for sports figures, entertainers and some of the top network marketers from around the world, including the site Downline University built around the concept of paying it forward.

In recent years, Richard helped take a traditional small business online and helped them generate sales in excess of 1 billion dollars in 2 years by applying simple but effective marketing strategies and automating the process. This book focusses on the business of network marketing, but the principles of the book apply to any type of home based business. It was this idea of creating a universal training system and the concept of **"Learn, Earn, Pay It Forward"** that lead to the development of top training website Downline University.

Our mission is to give our fellow network marketing community a strong foundation to help build their empires in today's ever-changing world of technology, help them become dominant players in the industry and mentor them to help change the perception of network marketing. Our industry of the home based business with the help of the internet is now converging globally into what we call Social Network Marketing. I'm convinced that Social Network Marketing is the only way people will build their financial empires now and in the future. Businesses that don't use this model will struggle and possibly seize to exist.

"YOU CAN NOW LIVE YOUR DREAM. IT ALL STARTS TODAY!"

For Over 20 Years
Newspaper, Television, Radio and Documentaries Agree
"Richard's Revolutionary System Works"

We Didn't Cold Call, Bother Friends & Family or Neighbors... *It Was All Automated*
We always get asked, "What if I try it and it doesn't work?" What if it works and you didn't try it?

Stay At Home Mom
Holly
Denver, Colorado
I didn't want anybody else raising my baby. My first month in and I can't believe how fast this grew. I share this with everyone I run into. It is so easy.

In The Military
CJ
Hawaii
Suplimenting my military income. Who you join with makes the difference whether you make money or waste time. I'll be seeing you at the top.

Corporate Lay Off
Olivia
After getting laid off from corporate America in the middle of our greatest recession, I didn't think I could find a job. Thanks to this opportunity, my financial future is all in my hands

Single Mom
Andrea
Denver Colorado
Tire of working all the time and not spending time with my children. I finally came across something simple. A few hours a week now pays my rent.

Factory Worker
Jorge
Oxnard, California
Have you ever been laid off during Christmas? I was, and it was a horrible. This system is making me money from home spending more time with my kids with no more stress.

I Was Sick & Tired of Being Sick and Tired
Brad
Making money in my first two weeks. I know I'm aboard the fastest income builder. I can only imagine how my income is going to grow exponentially, WOW.

Yoga Teacher
Britney
I've tried other home based businesses and all I ever did was accumulate debt. This has been an incredible experience. I'm now making passive residual income from home with very little effort.

Facebook and YouTube Makes Me Money
Kristen
I'm on Facebook and YouTube all the time. Now I found a way to make money while I'm having fun with my friends.

School Teacher
Michelle
I love what I do as a school teacher, but unfortunately we do not make much money. It's sad but true. Using this system gives me the financial relief to do what I enjoy best, which is working with children.

Our Members Succeed... Because We Automated The Duplication Process

About This Book

I want to start first by congratulating you on your new business venture and for purchasing **"Your First 90 Days in Network Marketing"**. I personally believe that we all want to make a difference in our lives and the lives of others. You may be marketing a product or service that makes a physical difference in people's lives, but in the end, we're all here because we want to make a financial difference.

We conduct presentations to thousands of people around the world at live events, and we always ask the following two questions (you can fill in the blank with your product or service).

"How many of you are here to learn more about the _____, please raise your hands." (you always get a few people that raise their hands). **Then we ask,** *"How many people are here to learn how to make more money?"*

Do you want to guess how many people fanatically raise their hands with excitement at the second question? ***Almost everyone!*** Take notice that we use the word **"learn"** in both those questions. **People want to learn!**

The one common denominator in this industry, is that people get all hyped up after enrolling at an event or home party and don't know what to do next. Most people in this industry are sponsored by someone that just previously enrolled and also has no experience as to how to build a network marketing business.

This book will not take you through the history of network marketing. We cover that subject in our other book **"The Ultimate Guide For Network Marketing"**. The book your holding in your hands was designed to help you build a strong foundation over the next 90 days. Why 90 days? 90 days is the point where most people give up. Most people give up because they over complicate this business, and they have not been shown an easy systematic way to duplicate themselves. Yes, I used the word **easy.** Just follow the **easy steps outlined** in the book and you'll be on your way to a lifetime of residual income.

PREPARE YOURSELF TO BECOME
UNSTOPPABLE

Enroll In Training and Educate Yourself

Before you sponsor anyone, you need read this simple book to its completion. It's a very fast read and is designed to help you create momentum in your new home based business. Once you've read the book, come back and review each section and use the forms provided to start documenting your success and your failures. **WHAT... FAILURES?** Yes, we don't live in a perfect world and it is important for you to document your progress so that you can share with your mentors what is **NOT** working for you so that they can help you succeed, and for you to share with your downline what **IS** working for you to help them succeed. Never complain to your downline, you will poison their dreams. If you have a problem with anything, complain up, not down.

Learn the compensation plan inside and out.

In the beginning, it's important that you know the entire compensation plan for your own reference, but don't expect to explain the entire compensation to your prospects. For prospecting purposes, you only need to understand the first 2-3 rank advancements or levels. All you need to show is how to make $500 per month, then $1,000 per month, that's it. If you start talking big numbers, most people will not understand or may feel it is not attainable by them... it's not a realistic income for them. Using large incomes in your presentation will open the door for your prospects to ask you that one question every new distributor fears.... **"How much money are you making?"**

Master a napkin presentation! We have several illustrated in this book. Learn how to present key points in 3 minutes or less. You will lose people's attention if you start rambling. Enthusiasm is important, but over explaining is fatal.

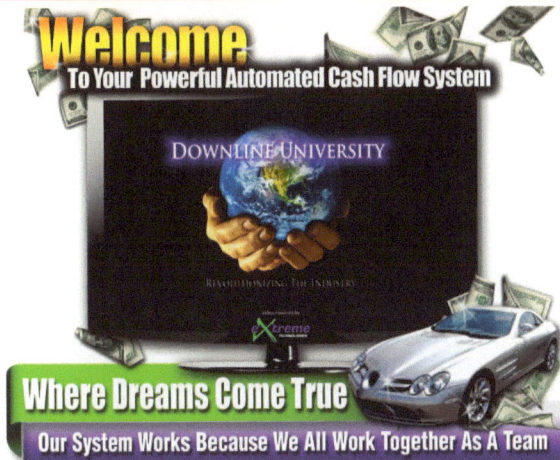

We are building a huge community and training library at **Downline University** to help our industry with innovative marketing techniques that will help you and your team duplicate your efforts both offline and online.

Downline University provides world class replicated web sites for your business and host a variety of marketing tools to help you market your business for little to no money at all. The web site has video training tutorials that show you step-by-step how to market your businesses offline and online, but mainly online, utilizing attraction marketing and social marketing techniques. We also share with you various sponsoring techniques to help you duplicate your business. Sharing this book and the website resources with your downline solves the problem of training your people 24/7 anywhere around the world from the day they enroll into your new business. In this business it is critical that you understand the process of duplication. You will never get rich retailing your product... **"Repeat after me!!...** *You will never get rich retailing your product."* You need to learn to sponsor people and to show your downline how to also sponsor and duplicate effectively. It's all about leverage.

Business Tip:

Never beg people to get into your business because you will be begging them to stay in. You need to have a big enough WHY to succeed at anything in life, especially if you want to change your lifestyle.

Know Your Upline

You're in business for yourself, but not by yourself. **You are not alone.** In our industry, if you don't make money, we don't make money. It is in our direct interest to help grow your business. It is imperative that you know your upline sponsors. Ask your personal sponsor for their contact information and do not hesitate to contact them for assistance. Your direct sponsor may not have the experience yet, but people above him do and are here to mentor you, and help you succeed.

My Personal Sponsor Is:

Name: _____

Email: _____

Website: _____

Phone 1: (_____) _____

Phone 2: (_____) _____

Upline Sponsor:

Name: _____

Email: _____

Website: _____

Phone 1: (_____) _____

Phone 2: (_____) _____

Upline Sponsor:

Name: _____

Email: _____

Website: _____

Phone 1: (_____) _____

Phone 2: (_____) _____

Upline Sponsor:

Name: _____

Email: _____

Website: _____

Phone 1: (_____) _____

Phone 2: (_____) _____

Business Tip:

If you're having a bad day, never consult with your downline, always speak to your upline. You will poison your business if you complain to your downline. Your downline can interpret your frustration as signs of quitting. You have the potential of shattering peoples dreams because something is not going your way. Do not be selfish, this entire business is built on team effort. Always be honest with yourself and do not confuse effort with results.

In order to make the money you're not used to making, you have to do things you're not used to doing. In the end, we promise you that it's all worth it. **The only way to fail is to quit.**

Determine Your WHY

WHY are you here? **WHY** are you really reading this book? **WHAT** motivates you? **WHERE** will you be in the next 3-5 years financially? **WHAT** would need to happen in your life to force you to make a change? **WHAT** has happened in your life recently that forced you to make a change in your lifestyle or priorities? If you don't make a change, will your life be the same, worse or better in the future?

You see no matter how much training you receive from us, no matter how many presentations you attend, there is one thing we cannot do for you. We cannot get inside your subconscious mind to force you to make a change. You need to determine **YOUR WHY**. You need to find the one thing that will give you the burning passion that will force you to succeed and to change your life.

You need to be crystal clear when determining your why and you need to write it down. If you don't write it down, it will never manifest in your life.

The price you pay for success, to change your life and to make your **WHY** a reality
IS NOT NEGOTIABLE,
if it is... it will never happen!

Write down your **WHY** on the front of a 3x5 card. On the back side of the card write down your personal mission statement. Carry it with you. Read it to yourself in the morning, and before you go to bed. If you're having a bad day, look at the card and it will remind you and help you get through the day.

"Make sure to write down your statements in the present tense. DO NOT use words like, "I would like to lose weight" always use words like "I am physically fit and feel great", "I am grateful for having an abundant life", "Business is always great". Doing this will invoke the Law of Attraction, and your higher source will see that you've taken action steps to force habitual changes and will attract events into your life like a magnet to make your WHY a reality."

Over the years, our members have shared their why's with us. Do any of these sound familiar? Dig deep and be honest with yourself.

I'm tired of going from job to job, I feel that I don't have many options.

I want to stay home with my children instead of sending them to day care everyday.

Even with a college degree, I still don't make enough money. I still owe over $80,000 in student loans.

I want to attend my kids sporting events without fear of losing my job.

I fear there will be no social security for me when I retire.

I want my kids to be the first in our family to go to college. I want to be able to give them a chance to do something extraordinary with their lives.

My 401k dwindled to nothing after 30 years of saving for my retirement.

I would love to have a vacation home for our family.

I want to help our church so they can minister around the world.

My spouse left me with nothing and I'm having to start all over again. I never want to have to depend on someone else financially.

I have a special needs child and the expenses are unbearable. I want to have the resources to give him a comfortable life.

My company keeps downsizing.

I'm tired of taking pay cuts while upper management keeps their current lifestyle.

I'm handicapped and regular jobs don't always accommodate for my needs. I know it's not their fault, but I need to find a way to take care of myself.

I hate driving in traffic everyday. My kids are asleep when I leave and going to bed when I get home.

I had a high GPA in high school, but could not afford to go to college fulltime. I know my parents tried to help and they did all they could. I want to make them proud of me and show them that even without college degree, I did make it. I want to take care of them in their old age, because they always took care of me, their retirement income will not be enough for them.

This economy has drained every penny I had saved for retirement. I have no choice but to succeed.

I'm a single parent and it's been very tough to raise my kids with not assistance from anybody. I am on the pursuit of happiness!

ROI (Return on Investment)

Breaking even is a critical step to making a six figure income.

When embarking on this journey to create a passive residual income, one must identify and break down how much product or business volume is required in order to break even. Most network marketing companies require a minimum monthly purchase in order to qualify for commissions. You need to understand that without products or services being sold, there are no commissions to pay.

Please refer to your company's compensation plan.

Most people when introduced to a home based business, get all excited, and are encouraged to place their first order of products and/or services before knowing the break even point.

We've designed a very simple form on the next page to help you find your ROI (return on investment). Knowing your expenses will help you when setting your financial goals. Anybody can set a financial goal, but without knowing the break even, how can you properly strategize to reach your goal?

Not knowing your ROI is like playing a game of darts in a dark room with the lights off. You will be throwing everything at the wall just hoping one will stick.

Turn on the lights because if you don't, one of those darts may bounce off the wall and hit you in the eye!

Breaking Even Is Your First Step To Making A Six Figure Income

How much is your monthly commitment? (or autoship)	How much does your product or service sell for?	How much is your discount in dollars?
$	$	$

If your discount is a percentage (%) this is how you calculate the discount. For example: a discount of 30% would be written as .30

So let's say your product retails for $100 and you get a 30% discount use the formula below to find out the discount in dollars.

Example:

Retail Price x Discount Percent = Discount in Dollars

$$\$100 \ \times \ .30 \ = \ \$30$$

A   **B**   **C**

$$\boxed{\$} \quad \times \quad \boxed{.} \quad = \quad \boxed{\$}$$

Retail   Discount %   Discount In Dollars

C   **D**

$$\boxed{\$} \quad - \quad \boxed{\$} \quad = \quad \boxed{\$}$$

Retail   Discount In Dollars   Your Product Cost

D

$$\boxed{\$} \quad \div \quad \boxed{\$} \quad = \quad \boxed{}$$

Monthly Minimum or Auto Ship   Your Product Cost   Quantity You Need To Sell To Break Even

Set A Simple Goal, Become A Sponsor

Goals are different from dreams or fantasies. I want to be a millionaire is not a goal. It is a dream or fantasy. I will be making $10,000 per month within 6 months is both specific to the dollar amount and a time line has been given. **That is a goal.**

Goals are measurable and in order to reach them, there are 4 important things to keep in mind and it's easier than you think.

1. Your desired goals need to be very specific and crystal clear.
2. You have to set a time line. (Realistic to you.) **MAKE A COMMITMENT!!**
3. Share your goals with your team. (We all want to see you reach your goals.)
4. You need to write them down or it doesn't count.

Your very first goal should be to get qualified to get paid.

Become a business builder in 7 Days.

Sponsor 2 People
As Soon As Possible

The Power of 2
is Exponential

Business Tip:

Do you want to reach your goals sooner than later? Get yourself an accountability partner, preferably in the same business. Review your goals and your **WHY** daily. In the beginning it seems like nothing is moving, but if you keep your goals close to you, you'll notice momentum in a short period of time.

Build A List

If your business opportunity was good enough for you, then there are over 380 million people in the United States alone that might think so as well. I get people all the time that tell me... **"I don't like talking to people."** or **"I'm not a people person."** I only have two responses for them. Either get over it, or go get a job. We are in the people business. We speak with people everyday of our lives, you might as well get paid for speaking. Get out your cell phones and open the address books, check your contacts in your e-mail program and start to make a list of people to introduce this wonderful opportunity.

Name	Phone Number	Email Address	Sit-Down	Presentation	Follow-up
1.			/ /	/ /	/ /
2.			/ /	/ /	/ /
3.			/ /	/ /	/ /
4.			/ /	/ /	/ /
5.			/ /	/ /	/ /
6.			/ /	/ /	/ /
7.			/ /	/ /	/ /
8.			/ /	/ /	/ /
9.			/ /	/ /	/ /
10.			/ /	/ /	/ /
11.			/ /	/ /	/ /
12.			/ /	/ /	/ /
13.			/ /	/ /	/ /
14.			/ /	/ /	/ /
15.			/ /	/ /	/ /
16.			/ /	/ /	/ /
17.			/ /	/ /	/ /
18.			/ /	/ /	/ /
19.			/ /	/ /	/ /
20.			/ /	/ /	/ /

The key is in the follow up. Follow up every 3 days after placing product or introducing the opportunity.

Sponsor Your First 2 People

The Power of

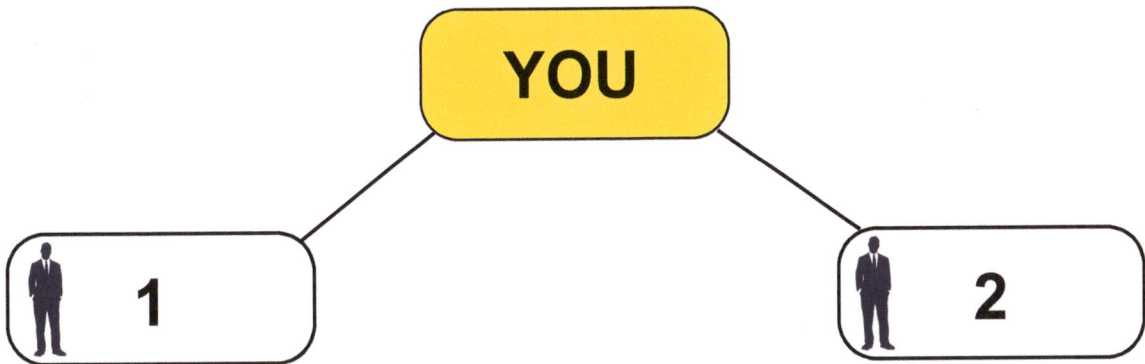

2

YOU

1

Name

2

Name

Build Your List

1._____   6._____   11._____

2._____   7._____   12._____

3._____   8._____   13._____

4._____   9._____   14._____

5._____   10._____   15._____

Take control of your business today.

Become a business builder simply by sponsoring 2 people. Take small steps and learn to duplicate. Work with groups of 2, help them become sponsors then move on to the next 2. Rinse, wash and repeat!

You Get Paid On The Effort of Others By Using The Principle of Leverage!

Pay It Forward To Create Your Own Momentum

Some people will tell you to sponsor as many people as possible, as fast as possible. I don't believe in that philosophy because I've seen thousands of people over the years build a house of cards that eventually collapses. You need to pace yourself first before creating momentum. Work with 2-5 people at a time and help them make money first. Unless you're very experienced, you need to learn to crawl before learning to run. This is not a sprint, it's a marathon. People that run marathons in this industry have a lifetime of residual income.

Show your downline what you know, share this book and become a teacher. The faster you become a teacher, the faster you will become a leader that people will respect and they will follow you to the top. This is all part of attraction marketing. Everyone wants to learn how to provide for themselves and for their families. There is a bible quote that goes as follows: "Give a man a fish and he will eat for a day, show him to fish and he will eat for a lifetime."

Because we are living in exponential times, I've changed it to say...
"Show them how to fish and your great grandchildren's, grandchildren will eat for a lifetime!"

The key to creating momentum is through the process of paying it forward. We all grow as a team, you can't do this alone, **it doesn't work that way!** Approach this business just as you would learning the art of self-defense. Just like a student in karate starts by learning the basic kicks, blocks and punches, before you know it, we will promote you to the level black belt, and the student then becomes the teacher.

Develop a Millionaire Mindset

Throughout my career, I've come to the conclusion over the years that there are only two types of people in the world. There are those that are rich and those that are poor. Which one do you want to be? Don't settle for second best. It's not that hard to make money in this industry, all you have to do is follow a proven system.

Don't hope results, **EXPECT RESULTS.** There is no such thing as luck. Create the results in your life, project yourself as successful, make it your entention that you will succeed. A paradigm shift will happen in your subconcious mind and you will begin to feel better, and as you do the pictures of your life will change.

Our business is 90% mental.

Over 25 years ago I used to do consulting work for the medical field and I would have to go into doctors offices to diagnose their computer systems. After a while people would forget I was there. It was interesting to hear the conversations around the offices. What was more interesting is that I would go back weeks and even months later... same stories and same drama. People complaining about issues in their lives with their spouse, family and friends. It's like I was in a time warp going back in time. Very few people would talk about the future and things they wanted to do or accomplish.

I mention this story because on occasion I've run into some of those same people... and guess what? **That's right... same stories, same drama.** But guess what? I've also ran into the others that did not feed into the drama that would

always talk about future events and their **WHY**. Those people actually moved on with their lives and many are living the lifestyle they talked and dreamed about. Somehow these things manifested in their lives. **How could this be?**

There are many studies proving that what we think about we bring about. That's why it is very important to take pen to paper and physically write down your goals and your **WHY**. When you write it down, your brain helps to visualize your desires and puts your words into momentum. The law of attraction is not some strange mental trick. Quantum physics today is proving that there is science behind this phenomenom.

In 1953 Yale University performed a study on its graduating class. The study asked a series of questions in regards to goal setting. They asked the graduates if they had planned out the rest of their lives and if they knew what direction they were headed. Interesting enough approximately 3% of the graduating class had actually written out a plan.

20 years later in 1973 Yale University made contact with the surviving members of the graduating class of 1953 for a follow up study. The original 3% of the graduates that had planned out their lives on paper were very well off financially. So much that their combined income was more than the income of the 97% graduating class **COMBINED!!**

You see, they graduated with a millionaire mind-set and they reinforced their thoughts and ideas on paper. It's a proven fact that something happens in your

brain when you write things down and attach emotion to your goals.

I can't stress enough for you to get a pad of paper and start writing down your life and business goals. Use the forms provided at the back of this book to give you a kick start. I can go on for hours on this subject, but I'll leave you with something that some of you might take interest in. It is on the topic of Mind Mapping, originally developed by Tony Buzan from the United Kingdom. His organization has been able to prove scientifically that our brains do not think linear. In other words, when we write down lists on paper, we tend not to finish everything on the list because our brain gets bored. We do not think in words, we think in pictures, use pictures as much as possible when writing down your goals and your why.

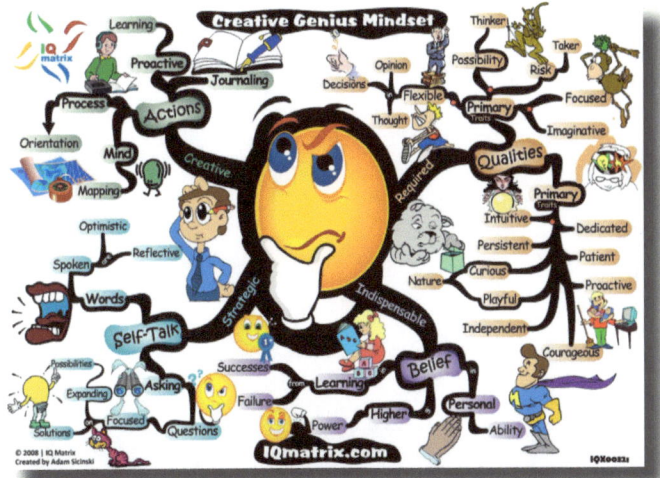

Try this experiment.

Close your eyes and imagine entering your garage and describe your car to me. Your mind will display pictures not words. If you have a red car, you don't see the word red, you see the color red. This is one of the many reasons people are taught to use dream boards to initiate the Laws of Attraction.

Mind mapping is a way to help both the right and left side of your brain connect which in return forces your brain to help you accomplish more.

The most recent version of Downline University and all my books were mind mapped on my iPhone in my spare time. There is a cool free version online at:

http://mindmeister.com

Contact and Invite

One of the biggest mistakes people make in this business is that they become secret agents. Nobody knows who they are, they go underground and expect their business to grow without them doing anything or ever talking to anybody about their product or opportunity.

The second mistake most people make is that they prejudge people. You simply don't know who will succeed and who won't during the first 90 days in the business. Over the years I've noticed some of the most unlikely people are the ones making multiple six figures per month. We have the tendency to target people that have sales backgrounds. My observations have also shown that sales people tend to always move on to what they think is the next best thing. Very few of them actually stick around to see it through to the end.

Then there's the really smart ones. Some of us try to sponsor people that are very smart thinking they will see the big picture with the big dollars and get all excited. Once again, my experience has shown that most smart people suffer from paralysis from analysis. They tend to over analyze everything to the point that they convince themselves that it's not going to work or that it will take too much work to make any money. If we are marketing a juice or vitamin, they will most likely find something in the product that they claim might hurt someone or that there is not enough scientific data. In all my years in the business I've never known of anybody ever dieing or getting sick from the results of product marketed through direct sales. People are so concerned on whether the products are FDA approved, **the FDA does not approve supplements.** It's funny how people are so concerned that your dietary supplements will do more damage to their body than the gallons of Starbucks they drink and the hundreds

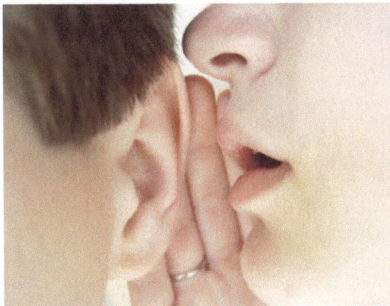

of pounds of In and Out hamburgers they eat every year. Pharmaceutical television propaganda in the United States has reached a new all time high with extreme fear factor marketing making everyone worried that they're going to die if they don't take their drugs when we get ill.

Have you ever watched and listened to the long legal disclaimers every time a new drug is advertised on TV? In the United States alone, people die every year taking drugs just as prescribed, yet if you're marketing a dietary supplement, many people will always ask you about the ingredients and the safety of consuming your product.

Average people just like you and me are the grass roots of this **$100 Billion Dollar a year industry.** You have to, and need to, get in the mindset of mentioning your business opportunity to anybody you make contact with. Don't be shy, because if you don't mention it to them, they will be mentioning it to you 3-6 months down the road and you'll be kicking yourself in the ass saying that you should have talked to them first. You never know if someone will say yes or no unless you ask. I'm not saying that you need to bug people to death and become the MLM Stalker. We don't know what financial issues someone might be experiencing, or if they have recently decided to make a change in their lives.

If you're using Facebook, MySpace or Twitter, please refer to our section on Attraction Marketing to make sure you do so in the proper way. You don't want to go on Facebook slamming everyone on your opportunity. You need to be careful on your approach or people will simply hide your friendship on their wall and nothing you say will even be displayed.

One more thing. Your business opportunity is not for everyone, and that is OK. **ACCEPT IT!!** Not everyone has the same wants and big enough why like you do.

It could be as simple as timing and nothing else. Just because they say no today, doesn't mean they won't say yes down the road. Another reason might be that not not everyone is willing to put a little effort every week to become financially free.

One reason 3% of the population makes all the money in the world is the simple fact that they or their families have residual income that has been accumulating and continues to grow exponentially over time. It may have taken them hundreds of years to get to this level, or like many people that I know personally, accomplished this over the last few years in network marketing.

> *Take the first step. You don't have to see the whole staircase, just take the first step.*"
>
> Martin Luther King, Jr.

So isn't it worth it to give it a shot?

Throughout this 90 day program, you'll notice that I keep addressing the issue of being in the right mindset and to take small measurable steps. **You need to have faith that the system will work.** You need to work the plan or you will be working someone else's plan for the rest of your life, just like the remaining 97% of the world population. Is that really what you want for yourself and your family? Of course not, that's why you took a step and purchased this book. You have a gut instinct that this can work for you... and it will.

In the 2006 film **"The Secret"**, co-author and success coach Jack Canfield used an example to help us visualize how our world unfolds in front of us every day.

Jack Canfield
Co-Author/Speaker
"Chicken Soup For The Soul"

"Imagine a car driving through the night, the headlights will only show 100-200 feet forward and you can make it all the way from California to New York driving through the dark, all you have to see is the next 200 feet. That's how life tends to unfold for us, if we just trust that the next 200 feet will unfold after that and the next 200 feet after that, your life will keep unfolding and will eventually get you to the destination of what you truly want."

We encourage you to visit: **www.JackCanfield.com**
In the area of personal development, few people in the world clearly explain why we do the things we do like Jack Canfield.

Network Marketing works the exact same way, follow the system and everything will start to unfold for you over time. In the end, don't over complicate the system and don't make it something that it's not. The product and company we market is the vehicle to help us obtain the lifestyle of our choosing.

Sooner than later you will have to interact with people and, ask your upline for help and have them work with you slowly by doing 3 way calls with your prospects so that you can learn from their approach. Don't feel intimidated that you might not be as good as your upline when presenting the opportunity. You will develop your own style over time.

The bottom line... don't be shy to approach anybody on your opportunity. Remember why you're doing this and don't let anybody steal your dreams...
especially the people around you!

The Secret Behind Attraction Marketing

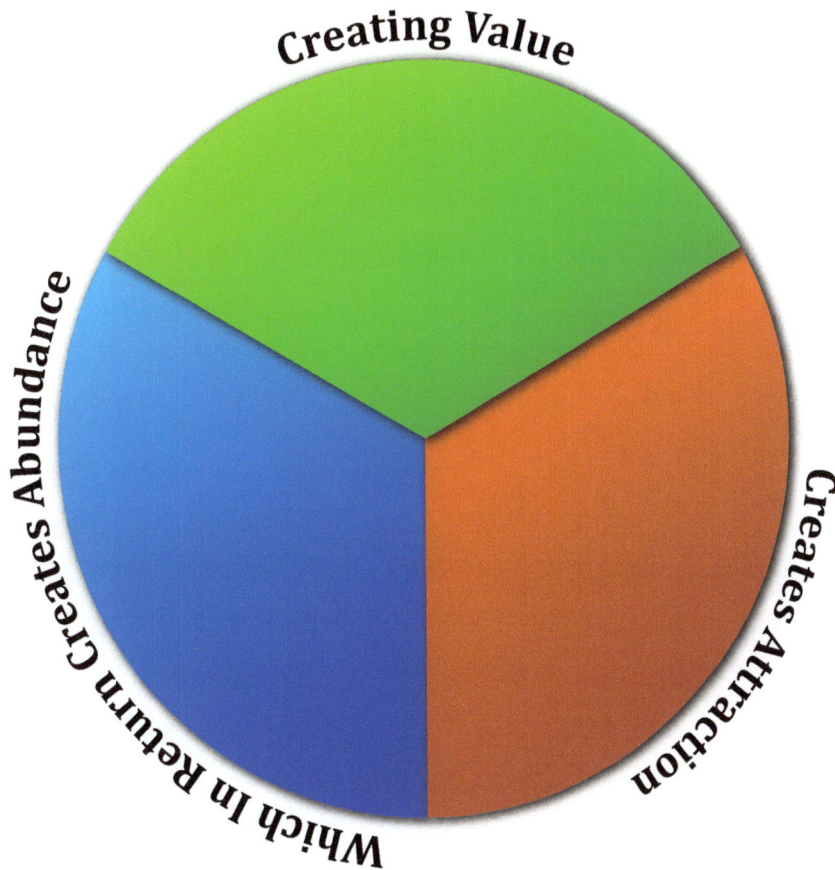

Creating Value

Creates Attraction

Which In Return Creates Abundance

Business Tip:

Important fact to remember. FaceBook has over 600 million users with over 5 million new users joining every week. They are expected to hit 1 billion members in the near future. YouTube has over 1 billion views daily. How you present yourself in the Social Network arena can and will determine your success or existence in the business world.

Attraction Marketing

The Social Networking Phenomenon

With Attraction Marketing we're going to show you how to take advantage of FREE sites using the now popular Web 2.0 Social Network marketing technologies to drive traffic to your business or opportunity. At the same time making you an expert in your desired niche. You need to become a leader and not a follower. The faster you stop relying on your upline, the faster and fatter your bank account gets.

You see, it doesn't matter whether your lead capture system is online or home meetings. You still need to drive foot traffic or online traffic so people can see your presentation, opportunity, lifestyle or product. In our opinion you need to do both to reach the top levels in your organization the fastest, but this is not required, some of you will excel without ever doing a home meeting. In matter of fact, during the writing of this book, I used some of the basic techniques illustrated in the book to drive over 400 people into a business opportunity during the prelaunch of a new network marketing company in 30 days, during Christmas all online, no meetings.

In my professional opinion if you are promoting an online opportunity, you can probably double your enrollment by doing home or hotel meetings. **Think about this for a second...** how many people have you ever met in person that makes all their money online? You read and hear about them, but never actually meet them. They're virtual. Don't you think others would want to meet and ask questions if you were one of these individuals? Are you starting to get the picture here about Attraction Marketing? People seek those that bring value into their lives.

There is no such thing as clicking a button, and going on vacation unless you have a ton of money to buy into or build a system, and if you're already making multiple six figures, your probably looking for a way to make it easier for people in your downline to duplicate. In either case it still comes down to time or money. Both of which you're trying to acquire or else you wouldn't be reading our book.

Your going to get sick hearing this... **"In this business if you don't duplicate, you don't make any money."** Duplication is the key to your success. There is something about a face-to-face meeting either at a home or hotel that is very hard to do online unless you use a webcam. That electricity that is in the air when someone gives a powerful message is what people feed off of and is the essence of why social networks attract.

When using web sites and social media networks, do not over sell people on the opportunity. Simply mention what your doing... ie: Working on my web site, going through training, etc. People don't want to be sold, but they will follow your story over time. You will start to see a steady flow of followers that in return become customers. Do not spam the system by over posting. You will either get flagged by the system or by users of the network.

If you are interested in building a mega downline over time, study the illustration on the previous page, it will give you a greater understanding as to the formula we use to personally sponsor hundreds of people per month. When you provide something of value, people will follow and your audience will grow exponentially.

The attraction you create will manifest the abundance in your life.

Social Marketing Strategy

In today's world there are many ways to sponsor and promote your business. This book is not designed to replace traditional sponsoring techniques, rather to enhance your offline efforts. One of my goals is to help brand you as an expert and make you stand out as a leader. In our industry leaders discuss philosophies and ideas on how their going to help distributors that have a big enough **WHY**, and how to help those that are already successful become even more successful. They discuss things that bring value to our community. You will be mastering this strategy to the point it becomes second nature to you, just like breathing and walking. You don't think about it, you just do it.

Branding yourself the correct way will attract people to you like a magnet. Social marketing or what we call Social Network Marketing requires that you pay close attention to what you are talking about online. This is very important because most people in this world are followers not leaders.

We are going to teach you how to master Attraction Marketing and the Law of Attraction. We're going to teach you how to create value in your words by giving away professional advise, products or services.

Think about it... how many times have you seen an ad or video with people pitching their product like "Hi I wanted to tell you about this awesome product... please signup."? There is nothing of value there. It's by giving away good advise, a sample or service that you create followers.

When people are searching your product or service on YouTube or Facebook, they already know about the product or service, so why would you continue to talk about it. If you say the wrong thing or don't connect with the audience, all you're doing is redirecting traffic to someone else that does.

On social networks, people are looking for **"Who is doing what and how."** People are looking for leaders, not followers. People want to see how your building your business, their looking to see if they can pickup any tips that will help them make a decision on whether to sign up and with whom they should sign up with. By giving away **VALUABLE** information it portrays you as someone that is not selfish and is willing to pay it forward and willing to teach them to also become successful.

"If You Master And Apply The Following Statement I Promise
It's Only A Matter Of Time Before You
Will Be Making Multiple Six Figures Per Year."

"GREAT minds discuss ideas, **AVERAGE** minds discuss events, **SMALL** minds discuss people."

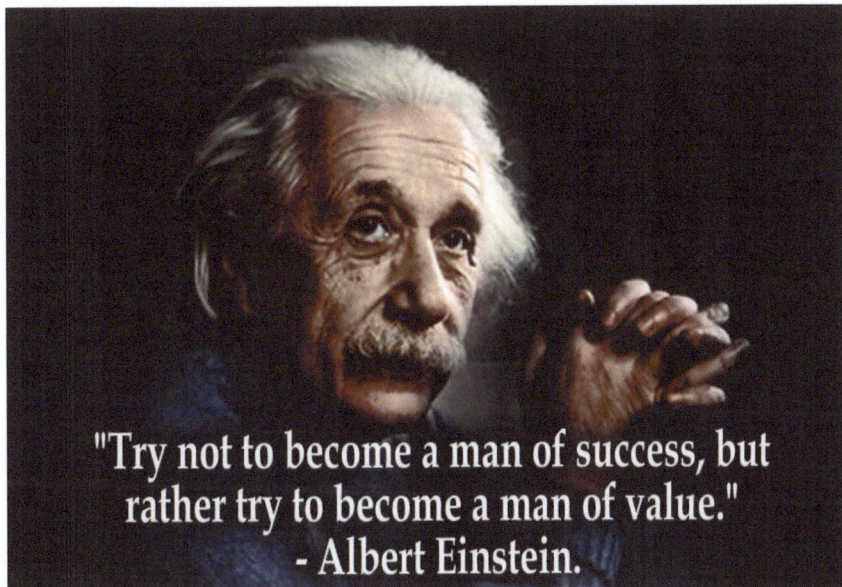

"Try not to become a man of success, but rather try to become a man of value."
- Albert Einstein.

Create Social Marketing Accounts

What we refer as Social Network Marketing simply means that we are going to show you how to promote yourself (YOU, remember?) On social networking websites like YouTube, Facebook, Digg, Hub Pages, Twitter, etc. Don't worry right now about how, just follow the instructions and you'll see over time that you will become an expert in your field and attract people to you and your business.

Go to the links below and create accounts. If you already have a gmail account, create a new account because you will be receiving lots of emails. We're going to setup an auto responder (vacation mode) to reverse market to people sending your sales information.

- http://gmail.com (create 5 accounts)
- http://youtube.com (create 5 accounts, use the 5 gmail accounts)
- http://facebook.com
- http://dig.com
- http://twitter.com
- http://hubpages.com

If you belong to other social network websites it's ok, we are going to focus on these for now. You can follow the same techniques on the other websites by yourself. In your back office to Downline University we list many of those social networking website links.

Gmail - Setting Up Reverse Prospecting

What is reverse prospecting? This technique has been used for years, but it is most effective when used discretely. After you set up your free **Gmail** account, you need to login into the account and click on settings at the top right of your screen.

Vacation Mode

Set the Vacation responder to on.
In the following fields enter something similar to this example:

Subject: RE: Thank You For Responding
Message:
Thank you for responding. I am receiving quite a few emails daily and will try to get back to you as soon as possible.

Our business is expanding and growing very fast and I take pride in personally training everyone on my team.

In the meantime please visit my website at: http://_____.com for more information.

You can also contact me on my personal email at: richard@_____.com
or call me at: 000-000-0000

Do you see what we're doing here?

You're only going to use this email to setup accounts and for a free auto responder that will solicit people for you automatically when they send you emails. When you setup accounts on certain networks, you will start to get solicitations from other network marketers that you will reverse prospect.

Set Marketing Goals To Fill The Pipeline

Before we start posting videos and blogging we must set some goals to keep track of our efforts. Make sure your goals are realistic to you. You can always revisit this page and update the information as you get better at social network marketing.

Goals	Goal Date	Goal Achieved
1. Generate My First 10 Leads		
2. Generate My First 100 Leads		
3. Generate 10 Leads Per Day		
4. Generate 20 Leads Per Day		
5. Generate 50 Leads Per Day		

The Fundamentals

It is better to start off slow and build a strong foundation. Pay attention to detail. You can add more strategies as you go along.

Now let's move on to YouTube. Make sure you use one Gmail account per YouTube account. YouTube does not allow you to get multiple accounts with single email address. That's why we had you create 5 Gmail accounts. One for each YouTube account.

A large part of your marketing will be on YouTube.com This website is visited by over 150 million Americans on a monthly basis, and it's free to use for advertising.

Become and leader by simply sponsoring 2 people into your business.

Become a Leader Maker

YouTube Campaign Strategy

Accounts 1-2
Will be used to post videos with keywords related to your business.

Accounts 3-5
Will be used to post videos using competitor keywords.

Everyone of your videos needs to have your website address and phone number in the description area. Very few people post phone numbers... guess what... it works, so get a voice mail if you don't want to take calls. Live calls convert 80% better than direct links to your website. On accounts 3-5 insert your competitors keywords, you'll use the same format except it will be primarily loaded with different keywords with a different title. When these videos show up on the competitions search, people will click on your link to see what you're all about. Below are examples of video subject line and descriptions. Don't copy verbatim, you need to make yours unique. Insert keywords in the description. **The names used here are for example purposes only.**

Your Primary Videos

Subject: Xowii The Best Opportunity Ever

Call me direct: 805-555-1212
http://_____.com

We have the best team in _____, team support is what it's all about. We provide you with all the tools and mentoring to succeed.

xowii energy
coffee fruit
xowii compensation plan
efusjon
xango

Your Secondary Videos

Subject: Xango The Best Opportunity Ever

Call me direct: 805-555-1212
http://_____.com

We have the fastest growing team in _____, team support is what it's all about. We provide you with all the tools and mentoring. Compare the pros and cons... it's not about the product, it's about who is going to help you get to the top.

xango energy drink
xango marketing
xango compensation plan
xowii energy
coffee fruit
xowii compensation plan

You don't need fancy equipment. All you need is an inexpensive webcam. Most laptops today have built in cameras. When you log into your YouTube account there is an option at the top right to upload or record a video. No fancy software is required, they provide everything you need online.

- Post videos twice per week.
- Record valuable useful information that will help your team grow.
- Use tips from this book in your videos and make them your own.
- Make sure to include your phone number and website link.
- Share on the video your why.
- Keep your videos shorter than 5 minutes. 3 minutes is best.
- State your phone number in the video when ever possible.
- Twice per week post positive comments on team member videos.
- Make sure your downline is commenting on your videos.

In the beginning doing all this seems awkward, but it works over time. Don't over analyze your video, just be yourself and talk as if you were talking to a friend. Always give professional advice and **ALWAYS EDIFY YOUR TEAM** and team leaders. People like to hear that you are in business for yourself, but not by yourself. When you edify, give credit and praise to people on your team, your are portrayed as sincere team player. Everyone wants to be on a winning team.

Don't be a goofball and run around in your pajamas saying you work in your bathrobe or something stupid like that. You would never attract someone like myself to listen to you or follow your videos. If you go that route, that's all you will attract. **Remember the Law of Attraction...** "What you think about, you bring about." Let people know you have fun, but serious about your business and your lifestyle, be honest and don't worry if you slip up, just hit record.

Facebook Marketing

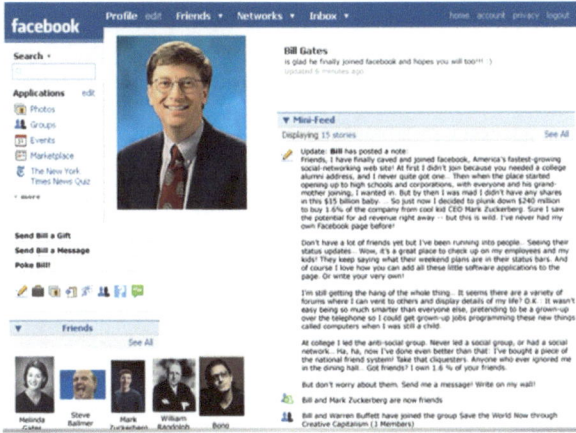

In the last couple of years, Facebook has gone from a college photo-sharing site to the largest social network on the planet. Facebook users can send each other a virtual drink, create and host events, advertise their businesses through social ads, and more.

During the writing of this book, most if not all readers are already on Facebook. You need to understand the basics of maneuvering through Facebook. Mastering Attraction Marketing in Facebook will make you a lead generating machine that will drive income back into your home based business. We make multiple six figures in income doing what we do. We've trained top producers in this industry to duplicate our system. Stay focussed on the task at hand. Revisit the chapter on Attraction Marketing before you start marketing on Facebook.

Follow the tips below, keep it simple, don't over think it!

- Post comments to your wall every couple days.
- Talk about what you're doing to grow your business.
- Give tips to your team on your wall.
- Refrain from talking specifically about your product when possible.
- Talk about your why and how you're motivated to reach your goals.
- If you talk about rank goals, share when you reach those ranks.
- Always edify the people you are working with, talk teamwork.
- Link videos on your wall after you upload to Youtube.

Linking videos is easy. To post a video on your wall, first find your video on YouTube and play your video. On top at the URL (web address), copy that link or below your video click on the SHARE button then copy that link. It's the same. Then log into your Facebook and start posting a comment about your video. Just above your comment is the word Link. Click on the word link then paste your video address in the box provided. That's it!

- **Have your friends and downline comment on your videos both on YouTube and on Facebook to start the wheel moving.**

Building a long term solid network through Social Marketing is all in the attitude and the intention of the words in your posts and videos. If you come off as a salesperson nobody will follow. Share your **WHY** and let people know why you do what you do. People love to help if they understand your **WHY**, and people will cheer you on as your business grows. As your team and others cheer you on, new prospects see that and it motivates them to take action.

As your business grows over time, many people that were sitting on the sidelines will come back later and ask you to show them how you did it. Everyone loves a success story that is sincere & honest. You will become unstoppable and inspire others to dig deep and find their **WHY**... and their **WAY**.

Everyone in the world hates relying on someone else (their job) to provide the income they need to survive in this world. Understanding the basic needs of the human race will help guide you through the social network.

Rinse, Wash and Repeat. Do these tasks every few days for the next 90 days!

Twitter

Of all the social networks, Twitter is the most misunderstood of them all. Twitter was first designed for people to broadcast a short 140 character message.

We're going to use Twitter for two things. First, we're going to use it for what it was designed for, to broadcast messages to our downline of upcoming events and second we're going to use this to help rank your videos and articles so that you can get more traffic to your websites.

Follow the tips below, keep it simple, don't over think it!

- Only post events such as conference calls and meetings.
- Every time you post a video on YouTube, announce it on Twitter
- Every time you post an article, announce it on Twitter.

That's it! Short and Sweet.

Twitter plays a bigger role once you hit the big money.

Once again, keep this part simple, you have better things to do. When you announce your YouTube videos and articles, it plays a part in getting your videos towards the top of YouTube. Google owns YouTube and likes it when you're promoting one of their products.

Hubpages & Squidoo Marketing

Hubpages.com and Squidoo.com are article submission directories. The majority of traffic and links are generated through article marketing. Most home based businesses, especially network marketers don't like writing articles and I understand why. It can seem tedious and you'll feel like you don't know what to write about. That's OK, it doesn't have to be perfect at first, just do it.

Before you begin to write an article, visit both of these websites and search for your opportunity by name. If you're in MONAVIE, BELLAMORA, XANGO or AVON, search by name and see how others are promoting their businesses. Write short 350-500 word articles about what your are doing to build a home business using the company you're involved with. **Remember,** not to over promote the company or the product. Trust me there will be thousands doing that. You need to stand out. You are here to promote yourself. Primarily mention your company or product in the title so that it comes up in the keyword search and once or twice in the article. I want you to talk about your **WHY, MISSION** and what your team is doing to build a home based business (insert YouTube videos). Place a link to your website or landing page on your **FIRST ARTICLE** on each network. On future articles place a link to your **ORIGINAL ARTICLES** on the opposite network. Over time, this technique drives tons of traffic back to you.

Follow the tips below, keep it simple, don't over think it!

- Post 1 article per week for the 90 days.
- Link future articles to the original articles you wrote.
- Remember Attraction Marketing. Remember Facebook.

Digg Marketing

Digg.com is one of the world's most visited social news websites and most important, one of the most indexed websites on the internet. Imagine that you own a company that just released a new product and wanted to let the world know about your product. Traditionally you would send out a press release and hope that the local news would pick up the story and write an article about your new product. Social news is like hybrid of a PR company.

From an outsider, you might think that Hubbpages, Squidoo and Digg are all the same, but to Google and all the internet robots that link up the millions of webpages from around the world, give Digg.com a priority.

Why is that important, you might ask yourself? Because on Digg.com you are telling the world about this cool article that you saw on Hubpages, Squidoo or YouTube, and **Google digs Digg.**

It may seem that you're going in a circle, and you are... a circle of profit. It's what we call the DU Factor over at Downline University.

Follow the tips below, keep it simple, don't over think it!

- Every time you write an article, make a simple announcement on Digg.

That's it! Short and Sweet.

Utilize Generic Replicated Web Sites

The reason our replicated web sites at downlineuniversity.com are so effective is because they are designed to capture the visitors attention using Attraction Marketing techniques. Company web sites for the most part are designed to only talk about the company, product and compensation. Most companies will not let you design a web site around their product due to the fact they would have to approve hundreds if not thousands of sites on a monthly basis. Companies are worried to death that if you build a website or blog with the wrong information or medical claims that the FTC might come down hard on them with fees and threats of shutting them down. Especially if you are in the wellness industry. You need to remember who spends millions of dollars on lobby groups in the United States... Pharmaceuticals! Those large companies don't want any competition, they want to keep everyone drugged up on their products.

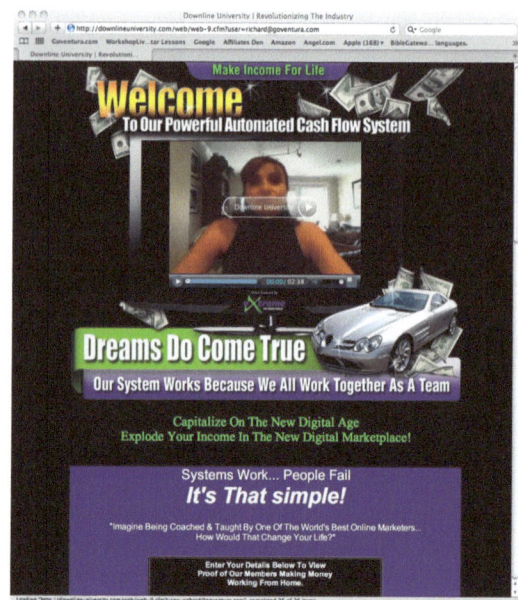

Only send people to your company replicated site to learn about the product once you've spoken to them in person or on the phone or captured their information on a form.

You need to remember and understand this statement. The company and products you are representing are strictly a vehicle to get you to your destination. Our web sites are designed to sell a lifestyle or business opportunity. At the end of the day, we're all here to make money. We could be selling staplers and

paper clips and our web sites will still convert website visitors to sales. Why? Because people ultimately will join your opportunity because they too have a dream and are looking to make a change in their lives.

If you don't have a replicated website that is filling the needs of the internet audience and/or promoting a lifestyle change, then visit Downline University. We're adding close to 200 replicated web sites, blogs and sales pages with various themes for you to customize.

The simplest way to utilize our sites is for you to register a domain name at GoDaddy.com. Domains there usually cost approximately $9 per year for dot com and .89 cents for dot info domains. There is also a video at Downline University that shows you how to register and forward your new domain to one of our replicated web sites.

When a potential lead visits your web site, they will have the option to enter their personal information. Once they enter their information and press submit, they are sent to a thank you page. You then are sent the lead information as the customer is sent a thank you email. This is what is called a simple auto responder. At Downline University, we also provide to our members our entire email marketing campaign that we use every day to sponsor people into network marketing companies. You can either use these email auto responders campaigns with your own software or use Aweber or iContact. Both Aweber and iContact charge anywhere from $9 to $19 per month to auto pilot your email marketing campaigns.

Once you get the lead, it is imperative that you contact that person immediately to see if you can answer any questions. The longer you take to follow up, the colder the lead gets. People sometimes surf the internet for business opportunities and will forget which web sites they've visited. We convert hundreds of people because we call them right away.

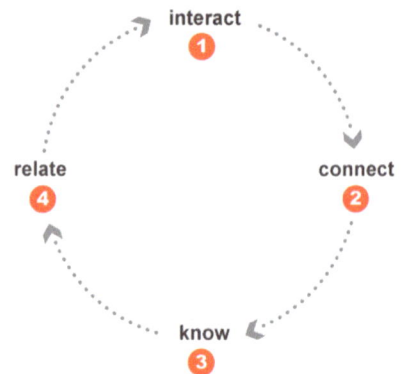

interact
1

connect
2

relate
4

know
3

I recently re-tested our replicated websites with a new MLM, in a segment where I had no experience (cosmetics), and enrolled over 400 people in 30 days using our Attraction Marketing system driving all the traffic to a replicated website. The key was in the follow up. I made sure everyone received 2 to 3 emails after they requested information from me.

"The Key Is In The Follow-Up"

Follow-Up & Handling Objections

Most people can double their enrollments if they simply follow up on their prospects. Such a simple concept, yet this is the number one fault of new distributors.

After you've shown or talked to someone about the opportunity, put them down on a schedule to follow up. Don't expect them to call you, they usually don't unless you happened to have dazzled them with your presentation, or the product gave them instant results.

Follow up on with your prospect 2-3 times over the next week. Don't bug them, simply call them for a follow up, ask them how they liked the product.

Always ask POSITIVE guided questions like:

I'm looking for some **positive** feedback, what did you **like** best about the business opportunity or product?

If all you had were a few hours per week to build a business, how much money per week would you need to earn to make it worth your time?

Talk to them about your **WHY,** and find out if they have a **WHY.** If they don't suggest ideas to them, most people want a change in their lives but have never shared it with anyone.

These sample scripts can be modified for e-mail, in person, phone follow up conversation or voice mail.

Hi (_____)

I was just doing a quick follow up to see what you thought about our new business, I would really love to see you come on board with us. It's a great opportunity and I'm on board a team with easy to use tools to help our business grow. We're also backed by a multi-million dollar company.

As I mentioned, we provide training and mentoring to get you in the money fast. If you have 3 minutes, I can get you started on some training now. Let me guide you through the sign up process on my website since you'll be doing the same with your own people. You'll see how easy it is to enroll in our business.

Hi (_____),

I just wanted to give you a quick update on my business. I love it! It allows me the freedom to take care of my children and do my marketing on a part time basis from home. Our team has the best tools 24/7. But like anything else if you don't take advantage of them they won't do you any good!

Take a look at my web site, give me a call, I would love to have you on my team. I would love your feedback. Have a great day, Bye for now

Business Tip:
Another suggestion when developing your own style. When talking to people try and mention to them about First Movers Advantage. People are enrolling every minute of the day. The faster you enroll, the faster your business will start to grow. At the rate that we're going if you don't enroll now, your friends and family will be trying to enroll you down the road.

Hi guys (your name) here!

All I can say is **WOW!** If you don't like to be challenged or pushed this isn't the team for you! You have to be willing to dedicate 90 days working your business for this to work for you. I learned something over the years if you give something hobby efforts you get hobby results. So if you are willing to give this 100% effort you will love my team!

Give me a call lets chat.
Have A Great day, Bye for now

_____

Hi (_____),

I wanted to share with you the reason I got into this business. I have a pretty big why and I'm determined to contribute to my family's financial situation while I stay home with the kids. You have to be willing to work your business everyday even if it is for 15 minutes for the next 90 days. They call this filling your funnel. If you don't you won't get leads, you won't grow, you won't see community results and you will give up! See, when you help others and pay it forward, you start to develop the snowball effect and it gets bigger and bigger.

So if you want to join a fast growing team with a lot of momentum, give me a call. Have a great Day.

I will talk to you soon.

Most Common Objections

Objection: "My monthly auto ship is too expensive."

Answer: "What if I can show you how to get your product for FREE?"
Your objective as a sponsor should be to help your downline get their product for free over a short period of time. Calculate how many people they need in their downline to get their product covered and help them layout some sponsoring goals. Make sure to give yourself a timeline and commit to helping them, show them how to duplicate!

Objection: "I can get a similar product for a lot less money at Costco."

Answer: "There might be similar products on the market. Our product may or may not be the lowest priced on the market. We are a distribution channel and our company ships millions of dollars of product every week. Does Costco or Walmart pay you a referral fee every time you send someone to their store... **probably not.**"

Don't get into a pissing contest on who's product is better or cheaper. It's a no win scenario with certain people. We get paid to market products via direct sales. Paperclips or Juice... it doesn't matter. The product is the vehicle and we are the distribution channel.

Objection: "I don't have enough time?"

Answer: "How much time do you think it's going to take?"
Answer: "How much money per week would make it worth your time?"
Answer: "That's exactly why I got involved, because I didn't seem to have enough time to spend with my family and friends. Now my friends and family all work together on this new venture with me. We're spending time together having fun making money."

Business Tip:
Focus on the positive. There is no such thing as a perfect company or perfect product. Work with what you have and enjoy the process. As you build your business and become proficient at Attraction Marketing, your business will continue to grow steadily and the objections will seem to disappear over time. Have confidence.

What can I say... we live in a very negative society. It's no mistake that only 3% of the population makes 97% of all the income in the world.

You have decided to get involved in a multi-million dollar business opportunity. Not everyone you run into will have the same wants and desires that you have. Some people like your friends and family are usually the first to give you grief about this new business.

Most of the time they're trying to protect you because maybe they've tried something in the past and it didn't work out for them. With others it's because they don't like people succeeding at something while their stuck at their dead end jobs. You'll be surprised how much jealousy will cross your path.

Over the years, I've done some exhaustive surveys with many current and former network marketers. For those former network marketers that never made any money or quit after a short period of time the results pretty much landed into two categories.

Category One: It's a scam, Those Things Never Work, I Got Ripped Off
After investigating deeply into their activities, the final result was always the same. Either they never followed a system or the time they claimed to have spent every week working the business was nowhere near what they originally claimed. If you're committing to 3 hours per week, make sure it's a solid 3, not 3 hours watching your kids or TV trying to build a business all at once.

Category Two: My Sponsor Went Into The Witness Protection Program

This one really baffle's me, because those sponsor's that disappear once you sign up don't realize how much money they could be making if they just provided a little support. This is why you need to know your upline 4 levels up.

The moral of the story is to study the compensation plan, talk to your upline, get plugged into the system, know your product and don't worry about objections.

Life is full of excuses and it's not always the right time for everyone. Remember that you have a bigger **WHY** than most people and part of our job is to find like minded people.

Someone that tells you "No" today, will not necessarily mean "No" tomorrow.

"A good objective of leadership is to help those who are doing poorly to do well and to help those who are doing well to do even better."

Jim Rohn

Duplicate Yourself

Remember what we said in the beginning? You will never get rich retailing your product. You need to sponsor people and teach them to duplicate.

Don't reinvent the wheel. This is a copy cat business. Have your downline follow every step as outlined just for you. Once they get the hang of the entire program, they can if they wish alter or customize to their personal needs. Talk to them about what's worked and what hasn't worked. Have them go through each step. What didn't work for you might work for them. Our system is proven and is in use everyday by thousands of home business owners around the world.

Repeat all the steps in this book over the next 90 days. 90 days in this business is critical to your success. Remind yourself that network marketing is not a get rich quick scheme. It is a journey, a marathon, not a sprint. In order for you to be making the money you're not used to making, you need to do things you're not used to doing.

Remember your **WHY.**

Sponsor 2 People
As Soon As Possible

The Power of 2
is Exponential

Napkin Presentations (Bonus Chapter)

If you're doing one on one sessions with your prospects it is imperative that you master a napkin presentation or elevator pitch. If it takes you longer than 2-3 minutes to explain your business opportunity, you shouldn't do it at all.

Napkin presentations have been used over the years due to the fact that many one on one business opportunity meetings are done at coffee shops. People would pickup up napkins and start drawing their compensation plans and their marketing strategies.

Sticking to our Attraction Marketing principles, I rarely draw the compensation plan on a napkin. It's too complicated to explain in 3 minutes, I personally use napkin presentations to demonstrate our philosophy on how we make money from home. I start by sharing my **WHY** and then proceed to teach them about leverage. **Whenever possible, I have them draw out the presentation.** If you keep it simple, they can use stick drawings, the quality is not important here. When someone writes anything down on paper, the brain makes a connection you'll commit it to memory and they begin to relate.

When I'm done with the napkin presentation they will either sign up on the spot or go home wondering about their job security. If they are on the run or seem distracted, I'll ask for an appointment and move on.

Remember not to over sell, a napkin presentation is designed to pique their interest and for you to identify tire kickers from those that genuinely are seeking to change their lifestyle. Memorize and make them your own to fit your situation.

Over time create your own 3-5 napkin presentations.

This next napkin presentation is used when I might be explaining residual income and the power of leverage.

Napkin Presentation #1

Let me ask you something, in life, there is one thing that we all seem to want more of... Time & Money am I correct?

Most people are on the 40/40/40 plan. Work 40 hours per week for 40 years and retire on 40% of their income. If people can barely survive on 100% of their current income, how do you think they will ever survive on 40%?

Our business works very similar to a real estate brokerage. In a real estate office there is a broker of record. The broker can't handle all the deals so he hires on agents. The broker has a commission split with his agents on every deal they close. Our business is similar with one exception. You see the broker wants to leverage his time with the agents. The more agents he brings in the more money he makes.

But there is a problem with this business model.

Agents will eventually want to make more money and will want to become Brokers themselves or they will constantly be asking for higher commission splits. Eventually another broker can offer them a higher split, and if they are not loyal to you or your company, they will leave for a higher pay day.

Others might leave to open their own offices and **YOU HAVE NOW TRAINED YOUR COMPETITION.** They know how you market to get clients and they will use it to compete against you. You're now back to hiring more agents and the your stuck in the self-employed rat race.

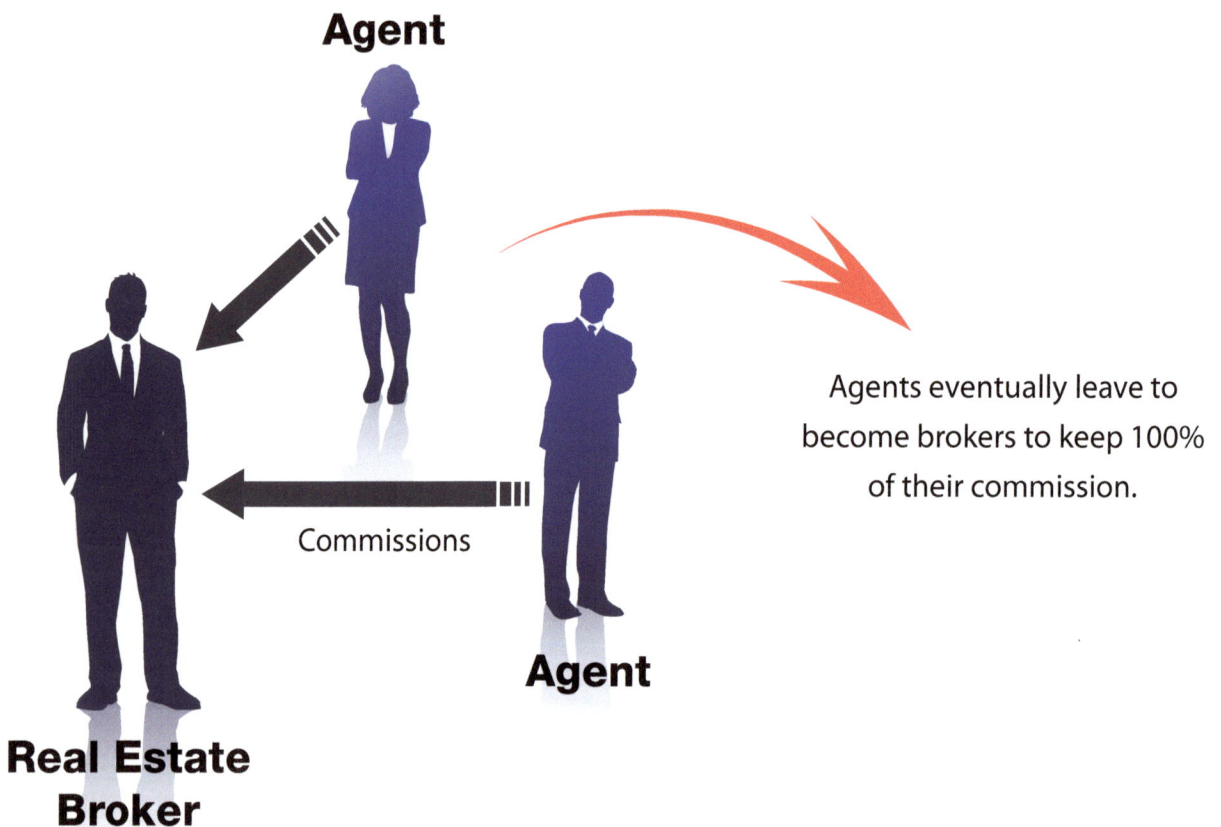

Agent

Agents eventually leave to become brokers to keep 100% of their commission.

Commissions

Agent

Real Estate Broker

In our business, we leverage time and people but there is no income cap and people are encouraged to make as much money as they desire. We get paid residuals on the team total. My associates can actually surpass me in rank and income, but I will always make a residual check on the effort of the entire team.

At my current job, my boss will never want me making more money than him. Here it's actually encouraged and I'm in business for myself, but not by myself.

Our Business Model

We All Win
Imagine Being A Stock Holder in Starbucks
Receiving Residuals on Every Cup Of Coffee Sold Worldwide

Napkin Presentation #2

Let me ask you something, in life, there is one thing that we all seem to want more of... Time & Money am I correct?

My associates and I train and mentor people that work from home to get better organized. We help structure their business so that they work less hours over time. Your income grows because we show you how to leverage.

Don't you think you work just as hard as a millionaire? Sure you do!

Making a lot of money has nothing to do with your education. Fact is most people in the United States work for college drop outs and most people with college degrees don't even work in the field they studied in college.

People that make a lot of money learn to build a foundation that allows them to do what they want with their time. We have a system that is time tested and proven. **The only way to fail is to quit.**

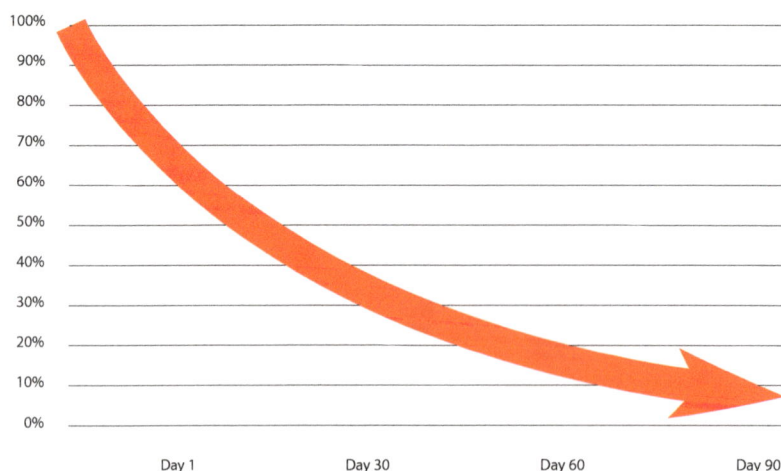

Time Spent Sponsoring

Summary

We started this journey talking about determining your **WHY**. Throughout the book we made dozens of references about your **WHY** to help motivate and push you through the small hurdles of building a successful social network marketing business. **This business is 90% mental.**

I'm always amazed at the capabilities people have, but disappointed at what they're willing to risk to obtain their goals and dreams. I know people that will spend $10 on Starbucks everyday but will not spend a dime to improve their lives. I know people that drive 2 hours a day in congested freeways in Los Angeles to get to work, they complain everyday about their jobs, but won't take the steps necessary to get them out of that situation.

This is an easy business but you need to understand that there is a process to get you making money. Part of that process could mean you have to jump a few hurdles and you might have to face some fears that you may have.

Let me pose a few questions that will get you thinking.

Question #1

If I wrote you a check for $100,000 every month for a year and all you had to do is generate some leads and sponsor 40 people per month. How hard would you work to make sure you completed your tasks?

Question #2

If I put a plank between the roof tops of two 15 story buildings and gave you 3 minutes to go across to the adjacent building and waiting for you on the other side was $10,000 in cash, would you walk the plank. **The catch:** building number 2 is on fire and will collapse within 20 minutes.

Question #3

If I put a plank between the roof tops of two 15 story buildings and gave you 3 minutes to go across to the adjacent building and waiting for you on the other side was your son or daughter. Would you walk the plank to bring them back. **The catch:** building number 2 is on fire and will collapse within 20 minutes.

Do you see where I'm going with this? It's all about how much value your mind associates with each one of those scenarios.

You see perception and value is in the eye of the beholder. Most people will never reach their goals because they haven't put enough feelings behind their intentions. Most people are spectators in the game of life and in order to have a chance of winning, you actually have to play the game.

A persons net worth can usually be measured by the amount of uncertain risk they are willing to live with. Most people wait until they have nothing before they make their move. It's at that point of having nothing that they redefine their **WHY** and suddenly their perception changes.

I've personally met people that were living in their cars that are now making multiple six figures running a home based business. They attached so much feeling behind their **WHY** everyday that it transformed their lives instantly.

People always ask, **"What if I try it and it doesn't work?** I always answer, **"What if it works and you didn't try it?"**

YOUR WHY IS THE FUEL TO BECOME
UNSTOPPABLE

Coming Soon To A Book Store Near You

There may come a time when you will want to kick it up a notch. Our insider secrets of internet marketing millionaires will help you take your game to the next level with easy to understand step-by-step visual tutorials.

Here is a sneak peek of what you will find in our **XFACTOR SERIES.**

Vol. 1 Wordpress For Social Network Marketing

Vol. 2 Wordpress Plugins to Automate Your Business

Vol. 3 The Ultimate Link Juice

Vol. 4 Multiple Sources of Income

Vol. 5 Blogging For Profit

Vol. 6 Social Network Marketing

Vol. 7 List Building

Vol. 8 Creating Your Own Product

Vol. 9 How To Have a Successful Product Launch

Vol. 10 Launching A Membership Website

DOWNLINEUNIVERSITY™

www.DownlineUniversity.com

Your Commitment Your WHY

A critical part of your success is being able to write down your WHY, your short and long term goals.
Be crystal clear, make sure they are measurable and give yourself a timeline.

What is you **WHY?**

The reason I have chosen to start my new home business is...

Starting my new business venture is important to me because...

Visualizing achieving my accomplishment makes me feel...

When I realize my dream, I will be able to help the following people or groups...

Your Commitment Your Goals

A critical part of your success is being able to write down your WHY, your short and long term goals.

Be crystal clear, make sure they are measurable and give yourself a timeline.

Short Term GOALS (within 90 days)

Goals	Target Date	Date Completed

Long Term GOALS (beyond 6 months)

Goals	Target Date	Date Completed

Memory Joggers

Remember to go through your email contact list and your cell phone address book.

Warm Market:
Address Book
Business Cards
Christmas Card List
Neighborhood List
College Friends
Co-workers
Old co-workers
Teachers

Relatives:
Parents
Brothers
Sisters
Aunts
Nieces
Uncles
Nephews
Grandparents
Grand kids
Father-in-law
Mother-in-law
Brother-in-laws
Sister-in-laws
Other in-laws

Who Is/Are My:
Accountant
Apartment Manager
Bus Driver

Car Salesperson
Chiropractor
Car Salesman
Card Group
Child Care Provider
Childhood Friends
Children's Friends Parents
Church Members
Club Members
Convenient Store Cashier
Co-workers
Delivery Person
Dentist Office Employees
Doctor's Office Employees
Donut Shop Manager
Dry Cleaner
Escrow Officer
Fed Ex Driver
Fireman
Fishing Buddies
Florist
Friends Housekeeper
Hunting Buddies
Insurance Agent(s)
Jeweler
Lawyer
Leasing Agent
Mailman
Maintenance Person
Minister(s)

MLM Friends
Neighbors
Optometrist
Paperboy
Pharmacist
Police
Property Manager
Real Estate Agent
Retired Coworkers
Retired Friends
Retired Relatives
Sports Team Members
Supermarket Managers
Tailor
Teachers
Truck Drivers
UPS Driver
Veterinarian
Waiters
Waitresses

Who sold me my:
Appliances
Boat
Business Cards
Camper
Car
Fishing License
Furniture Glasses
Contacts

MemoryJoggers

House
Hunting License
Office Equipment
Tires
TV/Stereo
Vacuum Cleaner
Wedding Items

I know someone who is a:

Antique Dealer
Art Instructor
Avon Rep
Bank Teller
Bus Driver
Carpenter
Chiropractor
Contractor Dietitian
Editor
Electrician
Fire Chief
Fisherman
Garage Mechanic
Golf Pro
Guitar Instructor
Interior Decorator
Karate Instructor
Lab Technician
Librarian
Lifeguard
Model

Motel Owner
Music Teacher
Musician
Notary Public
Nurse Office
Manager
Pilot / Stewardess
Printer
Restaurant Owner
Seamstress
Secretary
Security Guard
Sheriff
Student
Tupperware Rep

I know someone who:

Cuts My Grass
Delivers Packages
Dry Cleans My Clothes
Goes Bowling with Me
Hung My Wallpaper
Is in My Book Club
Is in Rotary, Lions
Is My Baby-sitter
Is my Barber/Hairdresser
Is my Former Boss
Is my Pastor
Is my Rabbi
Lives Next Door

Owns My Apartment
Painted My House
Repaired My TV
Sells Ice Cream
Sells Me Gasoline
Teaches Ceramics
Teaches My Kids
Was in my Car Pool
Was my Best Man
Was My Maid of Honor
Was My Navy Buddy
Was my Photographer
Was My Teacher

Home Meeting Checklist

The Most Successful Home Business Opportunity Meetins Host 12-15 People

To Do List
Prior To The Meeting

- [ ] Double Confirm Your Invitees
- [ ] Have a sign in sheet.
- [ ] Serve simple snacks (chips/salsa/water).
- [ ] No alcohol or BBQ, this is not a party.
- [ ] Keep room 70°-72°.
- [ ] Keep children in pets away.
- [ ] Have information, magazines, DVD's.
- [ ] Cue the DVD.
- [ ] Play living music as guest arrive.
- [ ] Keep volume low, don't talk over the music.
- [ ] Dress casual or business casual.
- [ ] It's normal for less people to show.
- [ ] Do not apologize for no-shows.
- [ ] Focus on the guests that did.

To Do List
During The Meeting

- [ ] **START ON TIME!!!**
- [ ] Only one person present.
- [ ] Have everyone silence their cell phones.
- [ ] Thank everyone for attending.
- [ ] State your name.
- [ ] Tell your story 3-5 minutes.
- [ ] Edify your team.
- [ ] Tell them you can answer question at the end of the meeting.
- [ ] Play the DVD or present live.
- [ ] Keep presentation to 40 minutes or less.
- [ ] You want a meeting after the meeting.
- [ ] Thank everyone again for coming.
- [ ] Thank the distributors that showed up.
- [ ] Answer questions and demo product.

Home Meeting Notes:

Home Meeting Tracker

Invitees

Name: **Rep** Guest
Phone:
Email:
Notes:

Name: **Rep** Guest
Phone:
Email:
Notes:

Name: **Rep** Guest
Phone:
Email:
Notes:

Name: **Rep** Guest
Phone:
Email:
Notes:

Name: **Rep** Guest
Phone:
Email:
Notes:

Name: **Rep** Guest
Phone:
Email:
Notes:

Name: **Rep** Guest
Phone:
Email:
Notes:

Name: **Rep** Guest
Phone:
Email:
Notes:

Invitees

Name: **Rep** Guest
Phone:
Email:
Notes:

Name: **Rep** Guest
Phone:
Email:
Notes:

Name: **Rep** Guest
Phone:
Email:
Notes:

Name: **Rep** Guest
Phone:
Email:
Notes:

Name: **Rep** Guest
Phone:
Email:
Notes:

Name: **Rep** Guest
Phone:
Email:
Notes:

Name: **Rep** Guest
Phone:
Email:
Notes:

Name: **Rep** Guest
Phone:
Email:
Notes:

Home Meeting Tracker

Invitees

	Rep	Guest
Name:		
Phone:		
Email:		
Notes:		

	Rep	Guest
Name:		
Phone:		
Email:		
Notes:		

	Rep	Guest
Name:		
Phone:		
Email:		
Notes:		

	Rep	Guest
Name:		
Phone:		
Email:		
Notes:		

	Rep	Guest
Name:		
Phone:		
Email:		
Notes:		

	Rep	Guest
Name:		
Phone:		
Email:		
Notes:		

	Rep	Guest
Name:		
Phone:		
Email:		
Notes:		

	Rep	Guest
Name:		
Phone:		
Email:		
Notes:		

Invitees

	Rep	Guest
Name:		
Phone:		
Email:		
Notes:		

	Rep	Guest
Name:		
Phone:		
Email:		
Notes:		

	Rep	Guest
Name:		
Phone:		
Email:		
Notes:		

	Rep	Guest
Name:		
Phone:		
Email:		
Notes:		

	Rep	Guest
Name:		
Phone:		
Email:		
Notes:		

	Rep	Guest
Name:		
Phone:		
Email:		
Notes:		

	Rep	Guest
Name:		
Phone:		
Email:		
Notes:		

	Rep	Guest
Name:		
Phone:		
Email:		
Notes:		

Home Meeting Tracker

Invitees

Name:	Rep	Guest
Phone:		
Email:		
Notes:		

Name:	Rep	Guest
Phone:		
Email:		
Notes:		

Name:	Rep	Guest
Phone:		
Email:		
Notes:		

Name:	Rep	Guest
Phone:		
Email:		
Notes:		

Name:	Rep	Guest
Phone:		
Email:		
Notes:		

Name:	Rep	Guest
Phone:		
Email:		
Notes:		

Name:	Rep	Guest
Phone:		
Email:		
Notes:		

Name:	Rep	Guest
Phone:		
Email:		
Notes:		

Invitees

Name:	Rep	Guest
Phone:		
Email:		
Notes:		

Name:	Rep	Guest
Phone:		
Email:		
Notes:		

Name:	Rep	Guest
Phone:		
Email:		
Notes:		

Name:	Rep	Guest
Phone:		
Email:		
Notes:		

Name:	Rep	Guest
Phone:		
Email:		
Notes:		

Name:	Rep	Guest
Phone:		
Email:		
Notes:		

Name:	Rep	Guest
Phone:		
Email:		
Notes:		

Name:	Rep	Guest
Phone:		
Email:		
Notes:		

Weekly Tracker

New Leads

Contacts Found Through Referrals/Presentations/Marketing

Name: _____ [Rep] Cust
Phone: _____
Email: _____
Notes: _____

Name: _____ [Rep] Cust
Phone: _____
Email: _____
Notes: _____

Name: _____ [Rep] Cust
Phone: _____
Email: _____
Notes: _____

Name: _____ [Rep] Cust
Phone: _____
Email: _____
Notes: _____

Name: _____ [Rep] Cust
Phone: _____
Email: _____
Notes: _____

Week Notes:

To Do List

Prioritize Top 3 Activities For The Day

Monday
☐
☐
☐

Tuesday
☐
☐
☐

Wednesday
☐
☐
☐

Thursday
☐
☐
☐

Friday
☐
☐
☐

Saturday
☐
☐
☐

Sunday
☐
☐
☐

Weekly Appointments

Month: _____

Year: _____

	Monday: ____	Tuesday: ____	Wednesday: ____	Thursday: ____	Friday: ____	Saturday: ____	Sunday: ____
	Appointments	Appointments	Appointments	Appointments	Appointments	Appointments	Appointments
8:00 a.m.							
8:30 a.m.							
9:00 a.m.							
9:30 a.m.							
10:00 a.m.							
10:30 a.m.							
11:00 a.m.							
11:30 a.m.							
12:00 p.m.							
12:30 p.m.							
1:00 p.m.							
1:30 p.m.							
2:30 p.m.							
3:00 p.m.							
3:30 p.m.							
4:00 p.m.							
4:30 p.m.							
5:00 p.m.							
5:30 p.m.							
6:00 p.m.							
6:30 p.m.							
7:00 p.m.							
7:30 p.m.							
8:00 p.m.							
8:30 p.m.							
9:00 p.m.							
9:30 p.m.							
10:00 p.m.							
10:30 p.m.							

Week Notes: _____

Weekly Tracker

New Leads

Contacts Found Through Referrals/Presentations/Marketing

Name: **Rep** Cust
Phone:
Email:
Notes:

Name: **Rep** Cust
Phone:
Email:
Notes:

Name: **Rep** Cust
Phone:
Email:
Notes:

Name: **Rep** Cust
Phone:
Email:
Notes:

Name: **Rep** Cust
Phone:
Email:
Notes:

Week Notes:

To Do List

Prioritize Top 3 Activities For The Day

Monday
- [ ]
- [ ]
- [ ]

Tuesday
- [ ]
- [ ]
- [ ]

Wednesday
- [ ]
- [ ]
- [ ]

Thursday
- [ ]
- [ ]
- [ ]

Friday
- [ ]
- [ ]
- [ ]

Saturday
- [ ]
- [ ]
- [ ]

Sunday
- [ ]
- [ ]
- [ ]

Weekly Appointments

Month: _____ Tuesday: _____ Thursday: _____ Year: _____

Monday: _____ Wednesday: _____ Friday: _____ Saturday: _____ Sunday: _____

	Monday Appointments	Tuesday Appointments	Wednesday Appointments	Thursday Appointments	Friday Appointments	Saturday Appointments	Sunday Appointments
8:00 a.m.							
8:30 a.m.							
9:00 a.m.							
9:30 a.m.							
10:00 a.m.							
10:30 a.m.							
11:00 a.m.							
11:30 a.m.							
12:00 p.m.							
12:30 p.m.							
1:00 p.m.							
1:30 p.m.							
2:30 p.m.							
3:00 p.m.							
3:30 p.m.							
4:00 p.m.							
4:30 p.m.							
5:00 p.m.							
5:30 p.m.							
6:00 p.m.							
6:30 p.m.							
7:00 p.m.							
7:30 p.m.							
8:00 p.m.							
8:30 p.m.							
9:00 p.m.							
9:30 p.m.							
10:00 p.m.							
10:30 p.m.							

Week Notes:

Weekly Tracker

New Leads
Contacts Found Through Referrals/Presentations/Marketing

Name:	**Rep** Cust
Phone:	
Email:	
Notes:	

Name:	**Rep** Cust
Phone:	
Email:	
Notes:	

Name:	**Rep** Cust
Phone:	
Email:	
Notes:	

Name:	**Rep** Cust
Phone:	
Email:	
Notes:	

Name:	**Rep** Cust
Phone:	
Email:	
Notes:	

Week Notes:

To Do List
Prioritize Top 3 Activities For The Day

Monday
- [ ]
- [ ]
- [ ]

Tuesday
- [ ]
- [ ]
- [ ]

Wednesday
- [ ]
- [ ]
- [ ]

Thursday
- [ ]
- [ ]
- [ ]

Friday
- [ ]
- [ ]
- [ ]

Saturday
- [ ]
- [ ]
- [ ]

Sunday
- [ ]
- [ ]
- [ ]

WeeklyAppointments

Month: _____   Year: _____

	Monday: ___	Tuesday: ___	Wednesday: ___	Thursday: ___	Friday: ___	Saturday: ___	Sunday: ___
	Appointments	Appointments	Appointments	Appointments	Appointments	Appointments	Appointments
8:00 a.m.							
8:30 a.m.							
9:00 a.m.							
9:30 a.m.							
10:00 a.m.							
10:30 a.m.							
11:00 a.m.							
11:30 a.m.							
12:00 p.m.							
12:30 p.m.							
1:00 p.m.							
1:30 p.m.							
2:30 p.m.							
3:00 p.m.							
3:30 p.m.							
4:00 p.m.							
4:30 p.m.							
5:00 p.m.							
5:30 p.m.							
6:00 p.m.							
6:30 p.m.							
7:00 p.m.							
7:30 p.m.							
8:00 p.m.							
8:30 p.m.							
9:00 p.m.							
9:30 p.m.							
10:00 p.m.							
10:30 p.m.							

Week Notes: _____

Weekly Tracker

New Leads

Contacts Found Through Referrals/Presentations/Marketing

Name:	Rep	Cust
Phone:		
Email:		
Notes:		

Name:	Rep	Cust
Phone:		
Email:		
Notes:		

Name:	Rep	Cust
Phone:		
Email:		
Notes:		

Name:	Rep	Cust
Phone:		
Email:		
Notes:		

Name:	Rep	Cust
Phone:		
Email:		
Notes:		

Week Notes:

To Do List

Prioritize Top 3 Activities For The Day

Monday
- [ ]
- [ ]
- [ ]

Tuesday
- [ ]
- [ ]
- [ ]

Wednesday
- [ ]
- [ ]
- [ ]

Thursday
- [ ]
- [ ]
- [ ]

Friday
- [ ]
- [ ]
- [ ]

Saturday
- [ ]
- [ ]
- [ ]

Sunday
- [ ]
- [ ]
- [ ]

Weekly Appointments

Month: _____   Year: _____

	Monday: ___	Tuesday: ___	Wednesday: ___	Thursday: ___	Friday: ___	Saturday: ___	Sunday: ___
	Appointments	Appointments	Appointments	Appointments	Appointments	Appointments	Appointments
8:00 a.m.							
8:30 a.m.							
9:00 a.m.							
9:30 a.m.							
10:00 a.m.							
10:30 a.m.							
11:00 a.m.							
11:30 a.m.							
12:00 p.m.							
12:30 p.m.							
1:00 p.m.							
1:30 p.m.							
2:30 p.m.							
3:00 p.m.							
3:30 p.m.							
4:00 p.m.							
4:30 p.m.							
5:00 p.m.							
5:30 p.m.							
6:00 p.m.							
6:30 p.m.							
7:00 p.m.							
7:30 p.m.							
8:00 p.m.							
8:30 p.m.							
9:00 p.m.							
9:30 p.m.							
10:00 p.m.							
10:30 p.m.							

Week Notes:

Weekly Tracker

New Leads

Contacts Found Through Referrals/Presentations/Marketing

Name:	**Rep**	Cust
Phone:		
Email:		
Notes:		

Name:	**Rep**	Cust
Phone:		
Email:		
Notes:		

Name:	**Rep**	Cust
Phone:		
Email:		
Notes:		

Name:	**Rep**	Cust
Phone:		
Email:		
Notes:		

Name:	**Rep**	Cust
Phone:		
Email:		
Notes:		

Week Notes:

To Do List

Prioritize Top 3 Activities For The Day

Monday
- [ ]
- [ ]
- [ ]

Tuesday
- [ ]
- [ ]
- [ ]

Wednesday
- [ ]
- [ ]
- [ ]

Thursday
- [ ]
- [ ]
- [ ]

Friday
- [ ]
- [ ]
- [ ]

Saturday
- [ ]
- [ ]
- [ ]

Sunday
- [ ]
- [ ]
- [ ]

Weekly Appointments

Month: _____   Year: _____

	Monday: ___	Tuesday: ___	Wednesday: ___	Thursday: ___	Friday: ___	Saturday: ___	Sunday: ___
	Appointments	Appointments	Appointments	Appointments	Appointments	Appointments	Appointments
8:00 a.m.							
8:30 a.m.							
9:00 a.m.							
9:30 a.m.							
10:00 a.m.							
10:30 a.m.							
11:00 a.m.							
11:30 a.m.							
12:00 p.m.							
12:30 p.m.							
1:00 p.m.							
1:30 p.m.							
2:30 p.m.							
3:00 p.m.							
3:30 p.m.							
4:00 p.m.							
4:30 p.m.							
5:00 p.m.							
5:30 p.m.							
6:00 p.m.							
6:30 p.m.							
7:00 p.m.							
7:30 p.m.							
8:00 p.m.							
8:30 p.m.							
9:00 p.m.							
9:30 p.m.							
10:00 p.m.							
10:30 p.m.							

Week Notes: _____

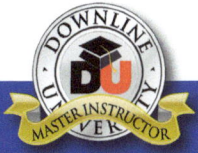

Weekly Tracker

New Leads

Contacts Found Through Referrals/Presentations/Marketing

		Rep	Cust
Name:			
Phone:			
Email:			
Notes:			

		Rep	Cust
Name:			
Phone:			
Email:			
Notes:			

		Rep	Cust
Name:			
Phone:			
Email:			
Notes:			

		Rep	Cust
Name:			
Phone:			
Email:			
Notes:			

		Rep	Cust
Name:			
Phone:			
Email:			
Notes:			

Week Notes:

To Do List

Prioritize Top 3 Activities For The Day

Monday
- [ ]
- [ ]
- [ ]

Tuesday
- [ ]
- [ ]
- [ ]

Wednesday
- [ ]
- [ ]
- [ ]

Thursday
- [ ]
- [ ]
- [ ]

Friday
- [ ]
- [ ]
- [ ]

Saturday
- [ ]
- [ ]
- [ ]

Sunday
- [ ]
- [ ]
- [ ]

Weekly Appointments

Month: _____   Year: _____

Time	Monday: ___ Appointments	Tuesday: ___ Appointments	Wednesday: ___ Appointments	Thursday: ___ Appointments	Friday: ___ Appointments	Saturday: ___ Appointments	Sunday: ___ Appointments
8:00 a.m.							
8:30 a.m.							
9:00 a.m.							
9:30 a.m.							
10:00 a.m.							
10:30 a.m.							
11:00 a.m.							
11:30 a.m.							
12:00 p.m.							
12:30 p.m.							
1:00 p.m.							
1:30 p.m.							
2:30 p.m.							
3:00 p.m.							
3:30 p.m.							
4:00 p.m.							
4:30 p.m.							
5:00 p.m.							
5:30 p.m.							
6:00 p.m.							
6:30 p.m.							
7:00 p.m.							
7:30 p.m.							
8:00 p.m.							
8:30 p.m.							
9:00 p.m.							
9:30 p.m.							
10:00 p.m.							
10:30 p.m.							

Week Notes: _____

Weekly Tracker

New Leads

Contacts Found Through Referrals/Presentations/Marketing

		Rep	Cust
Name:			
Phone:			
Email:			
Notes:			

		Rep	Cust
Name:			
Phone:			
Email:			
Notes:			

		Rep	Cust
Name:			
Phone:			
Email:			
Notes:			

		Rep	Cust
Name:			
Phone:			
Email:			
Notes:			

		Rep	Cust
Name:			
Phone:			
Email:			
Notes:			

Week Notes:

To Do List

Prioritize Top 3 Activities For The Day

Monday
☐
☐
☐

Tuesday
☐
☐
☐

Wednesday
☐
☐
☐

Thursday
☐
☐
☐

Friday
☐
☐
☐

Saturday
☐
☐
☐

Sunday
☐
☐
☐

Weekly Appointments

Month: _____ Year: _____

Time	Monday: ___ Appointments	Tuesday: ___ Appointments	Wednesday: ___ Appointments	Thursday: ___ Appointments	Friday: ___ Appointments	Saturday: ___ Appointments	Sunday: ___ Appointments
8:00 a.m.							
8:30 a.m.							
9:00 a.m.							
9:30 a.m.							
10:00 a.m.							
10:30 a.m.							
11:00 a.m.							
11:30 a.m.							
12:00 p.m.							
12:30 p.m.							
1:00 p.m.							
1:30 p.m.							
2:30 p.m.							
3:00 p.m.							
3:30 p.m.							
4:00 p.m.							
4:30 p.m.							
5:00 p.m.							
5:30 p.m.							
6:00 p.m.							
6:30 p.m.							
7:00 p.m.							
7:30 p.m.							
8:00 p.m.							
8:30 p.m.							
9:00 p.m.							
9:30 p.m.							
10:00 p.m.							
10:30 p.m.							

Week Notes: _____

Weekly Tracker

New Leads

Contacts Found Through Referrals/Presentations/Marketing

Name:	Rep	Cust
Phone:		
Email:		
Notes:		

Name:	Rep	Cust
Phone:		
Email:		
Notes:		

Name:	Rep	Cust
Phone:		
Email:		
Notes:		

Name:	Rep	Cust
Phone:		
Email:		
Notes:		

Name:	Rep	Cust
Phone:		
Email:		
Notes:		

Week Notes:

To Do List

Prioritize Top 3 Activities For The Day

Monday
- [ ]
- [ ]
- [ ]

Tuesday
- [ ]
- [ ]
- [ ]

Wednesday
- [ ]
- [ ]
- [ ]

Thursday
- [ ]
- [ ]
- [ ]

Friday
- [ ]
- [ ]
- [ ]

Saturday
- [ ]
- [ ]
- [ ]

Sunday
- [ ]
- [ ]
- [ ]

Weekly Appointments

Month: _____   Year: _____

Monday: ___	Tuesday: ___	Wednesday: ___	Thursday: ___	Friday: ___	Saturday: ___	Sunday: ___
Appointments	Appointments	Appointments	Appointments	Appointments	Appointments	Appointments
8:00 a.m.	8:00 a.m.	8:00 a.m.	8:00 a.m.	8:00 a.m.	8:00 a.m.	8:00 a.m.
8:30 a.m.	8:30 a.m.	8:30 a.m.	8:30 a.m.	8:30 a.m.	8:30 a.m.	8:30 a.m.
9:00 a.m.	9:00 a.m.	9:00 a.m.	9:00 a.m.	9:00 a.m.	9:00 a.m.	9:00 a.m.
9:30 a.m.	9:30 a.m.	9:30 a.m.	9:30 a.m.	9:30 a.m.	9:30 a.m.	9:30 a.m.
10:00 a.m.	10:00 a.m.	10:00 a.m.	10:00 a.m.	10:00 a.m.	10:00 a.m.	10:00 a.m.
10:30 a.m.	10:30 a.m.	10:30 a.m.	10:30 a.m.	10:30 a.m.	10:30 a.m.	10:30 a.m.
11:00 a.m.	11:00 a.m.	11:00 a.m.	11:00 a.m.	11:00 a.m.	11:00 a.m.	11:00 a.m.
11:30 a.m.	11:30 a.m.	11:30 a.m.	11:30 a.m.	11:30 a.m.	11:30 a.m.	11:30 a.m.
12:00 p.m.	12:00 p.m.	12:00 p.m.	12:00 p.m.	12:00 p.m.	12:00 p.m.	12:00 p.m.
12:30 p.m.	12:30 p.m.	12:30 p.m.	12:30 p.m.	12:30 p.m.	12:30 p.m.	12:30 p.m.
1:00 p.m.	1:00 p.m.	1:00 p.m.	1:00 p.m.	1:00 p.m.	1:00 p.m.	1:00 p.m.
1:30 p.m.	1:30 p.m.	1:30 p.m.	1:30 p.m.	1:30 p.m.	1:30 p.m.	1:30 p.m.
2:30 p.m.	2:30 p.m.	2:30 p.m.	2:30 p.m.	2:30 p.m.	2:30 p.m.	2:30 p.m.
3:00 p.m.	3:00 p.m.	3:00 p.m.	3:00 p.m.	3:00 p.m.	3:00 p.m.	3:00 p.m.
3:30 p.m.	3:30 p.m.	3:30 p.m.	3:30 p.m.	3:30 p.m.	3:30 p.m.	3:30 p.m.
4:00 p.m.	4:00 p.m.	4:00 p.m.	4:00 p.m.	4:00 p.m.	4:00 p.m.	4:00 p.m.
4:30 p.m.	4:30 p.m.	4:30 p.m.	4:30 p.m.	4:30 p.m.	4:30 p.m.	4:30 p.m.
5:00 p.m.	5:00 p.m.	5:00 p.m.	5:00 p.m.	5:00 p.m.	5:00 p.m.	5:00 p.m.
5:30 p.m.	5:30 p.m.	5:30 p.m.	5:30 p.m.	5:30 p.m.	5:30 p.m.	5:30 p.m.
6:00 p.m.	6:00 p.m.	6:00 p.m.	6:00 p.m.	6:00 p.m.	6:00 p.m.	6:00 p.m.
6:30 p.m.	6:30 p.m.	6:30 p.m.	6:30 p.m.	6:30 p.m.	6:30 p.m.	6:30 p.m.
7:00 p.m.	7:00 p.m.	7:00 p.m.	7:00 p.m.	7:00 p.m.	7:00 p.m.	7:00 p.m.
7:30 p.m.	7:30 p.m.	7:30 p.m.	7:30 p.m.	7:30 p.m.	7:30 p.m.	7:30 p.m.
8:00 p.m.	8:00 p.m.	8:00 p.m.	8:00 p.m.	8:00 p.m.	8:00 p.m.	8:00 p.m.
8:30 p.m.	8:30 p.m.	8:30 p.m.	8:30 p.m.	8:30 p.m.	8:30 p.m.	8:30 p.m.
9:00 p.m.	9:00 p.m.	9:00 p.m.	9:00 p.m.	9:00 p.m.	9:00 p.m.	9:00 p.m.
9:30 p.m.	9:30 p.m.	9:30 p.m.	9:30 p.m.	9:30 p.m.	9:30 p.m.	9:30 p.m.
10:00 p.m.	10:00 p.m.	10:00 p.m.	10:00 p.m.	10:00 p.m.	10:00 p.m.	10:00 p.m.
10:30 p.m.	10:30 p.m.	10:30 p.m.	10:30 p.m.	10:30 p.m.	10:30 p.m.	10:30 p.m.

Week Notes: _____

Weekly Tracker

New Leads

Contacts Found Through Referrals/Presentations/Marketing

Name:	Rep	Cust
Phone:		
Email:		
Notes:		

Name:	Rep	Cust
Phone:		
Email:		
Notes:		

Name:	Rep	Cust
Phone:		
Email:		
Notes:		

Name:	Rep	Cust
Phone:		
Email:		
Notes:		

Name:	Rep	Cust
Phone:		
Email:		
Notes:		

Week Notes:

To Do List

Prioritize Top 3 Activities For The Day

Monday
- [ ]
- [ ]
- [ ]

Tuesday
- [ ]
- [ ]
- [ ]

Wednesday
- [ ]
- [ ]
- [ ]

Thursday
- [ ]
- [ ]
- [ ]

Friday
- [ ]
- [ ]
- [ ]

Saturday
- [ ]
- [ ]
- [ ]

Sunday
- [ ]
- [ ]
- [ ]

Weekly Appointments

Month: _____   Year: _____

	Monday: ___	Tuesday: ___	Wednesday: ___	Thursday: ___	Friday: ___	Saturday: ___	Sunday: ___
	Appointments	Appointments	Appointments	Appointments	Appointments	Appointments	Appointments
8:00 a.m.							
8:30 a.m.							
9:00 a.m.							
9:30 a.m.							
10:00 a.m.							
10:30 a.m.							
11:00 a.m.							
11:30 a.m.							
12:00 p.m.							
12:30 p.m.							
1:00 p.m.							
1:30 p.m.							
2:30 p.m.							
3:00 p.m.							
3:30 p.m.							
4:00 p.m.							
4:30 p.m.							
5:00 p.m.							
5:30 p.m.							
6:00 p.m.							
6:30 p.m.							
7:00 p.m.							
7:30 p.m.							
8:00 p.m.							
8:30 p.m.							
9:00 p.m.							
9:30 p.m.							
10:00 p.m.							
10:30 p.m.							

Week Notes:

Weekly Tracker

New Leads

Contacts Found Through Referrals/Presentations/Marketing

Name: | Rep | Cust
Phone:
Email:
Notes:

Name: | Rep | Cust
Phone:
Email:
Notes:

Name: | Rep | Cust
Phone:
Email:
Notes:

Name: | Rep | Cust
Phone:
Email:
Notes:

Name: | Rep | Cust
Phone:
Email:
Notes:

Week Notes:

To Do List

Prioritize Top 3 Activities For The Day

Monday
☐
☐
☐

Tuesday
☐
☐
☐

Wednesday
☐
☐
☐

Thursday
☐
☐
☐

Friday
☐
☐
☐

Saturday
☐
☐
☐

Sunday
☐
☐
☐

Weekly Appointments

Month: _____   Year: _____

Time	Monday: ___ Appointments	Tuesday: ___ Appointments	Wednesday: ___ Appointments	Thursday: ___ Appointments	Friday: ___ Appointments	Saturday: ___ Appointments	Sunday: ___ Appointments
8:00 a.m.							
8:30 a.m.							
9:00 a.m.							
9:30 a.m.							
10:00 a.m.							
10:30 a.m.							
11:00 a.m.							
11:30 a.m.							
12:00 p.m.							
12:30 p.m.							
1:00 p.m.							
1:30 p.m.							
2:30 p.m.							
3:00 p.m.							
3:30 p.m.							
4:00 p.m.							
4:30 p.m.							
5:00 p.m.							
5:30 p.m.							
6:00 p.m.							
6:30 p.m.							
7:00 p.m.							
7:30 p.m.							
8:00 p.m.							
8:30 p.m.							
9:00 p.m.							
9:30 p.m.							
10:00 p.m.							
10:30 p.m.							

Week Notes: _____

Weekly Tracker

New Leads

Contacts Found Through Referrals/Presentations/Marketing

Name:	Rep	Cust
Phone:		
Email:		
Notes:		
Name:	Rep	Cust
Phone:		
Email:		
Notes:		
Name:	Rep	Cust
Phone:		
Email:		
Notes:		
Name:	Rep	Cust
Phone:		
Email:		
Notes:		
Name:	Rep	Cust
Phone:		
Email:		
Notes:		

Week Notes:

To Do List

Prioritize Top 3 Activities For The Day

Monday

- [ ]
- [ ]
- [ ]

Tuesday

- [ ]
- [ ]
- [ ]

Wednesday

- [ ]
- [ ]
- [ ]

Thursday

- [ ]
- [ ]
- [ ]

Friday

- [ ]
- [ ]
- [ ]

Saturday

- [ ]
- [ ]
- [ ]

Sunday

- [ ]
- [ ]
- [ ]

DOWNLINE UNIVERSITY MASTER INSTRUCTOR

Weekly Appointments

Month: _____   Year: _____

	Monday: ___	Tuesday: ___	Wednesday: ___	Thursday: ___	Friday: ___	Saturday: ___	Sunday: ___
	Appointments	Appointments	Appointments	Appointments	Appointments	Appointments	Appointments
8:00 a.m.							
8:30 a.m.							
9:00 a.m.							
9:30 a.m.							
10:00 a.m.							
10:30 a.m.							
11:00 a.m.							
11:30 a.m.							
12:00 p.m.							
12:30 p.m.							
1:00 p.m.							
1:30 p.m.							
2:30 p.m.							
3:00 p.m.							
3:30 p.m.							
4:00 p.m.							
4:30 p.m.							
5:00 p.m.							
5:30 p.m.							
6:00 p.m.							
6:30 p.m.							
7:00 p.m.							
7:30 p.m.							
8:00 p.m.							
8:30 p.m.							
9:00 p.m.							
9:30 p.m.							
10:00 p.m.							
10:30 p.m.							

Week Notes: _____

Weekly Tracker

New Leads

Contacts Found Through Referrals/Presentations/Marketing

Name:	Rep	Cust
Phone:		
Email:		
Notes:		

Name:	Rep	Cust
Phone:		
Email:		
Notes:		

Name:	Rep	Cust
Phone:		
Email:		
Notes:		

Name:	Rep	Cust
Phone:		
Email:		
Notes:		

Name:	Rep	Cust
Phone:		
Email:		
Notes:		

Week Notes:

To Do List

Prioritize Top 3 Activities For The Day

Monday
- [ ]
- [ ]
- [ ]

Tuesday
- [ ]
- [ ]
- [ ]

Wednesday
- [ ]
- [ ]
- [ ]

Thursday
- [ ]
- [ ]
- [ ]

Friday
- [ ]
- [ ]
- [ ]

Saturday
- [ ]
- [ ]
- [ ]

Sunday
- [ ]
- [ ]
- [ ]

Weekly Appointments

Month: _____   Year: _____

Monday: _____		Tuesday: _____		Wednesday: _____		Thursday: _____		Friday: _____		Saturday: _____		Sunday: _____	
Appointments		**Appointments**		**Appointments**		**Appointments**		**Appointments**		**Appointments**		**Appointments**	
8:00 a.m.		8:00 a.m.		8:00 a.m.		8:00 a.m.		8:00 a.m.		8:00 a.m.		8:00 a.m.	
8:30 a.m.		8:30 a.m.		8:30 a.m.		8:30 a.m.		8:30 a.m.		8:30 a.m.		8:30 a.m.	
9:00 a.m.		9:00 a.m.		9:00 a.m.		9:00 a.m.		9:00 a.m.		9:00 a.m.		9:00 a.m.	
9:30 a.m.		9:30 a.m.		9:30 a.m.		9:30 a.m.		9:30 a.m.		9:30 a.m.		9:30 a.m.	
10:00 a.m.		10:00 a.m.		10:00 a.m.		10:00 a.m.		10:00 a.m.		10:00 a.m.		10:00 a.m.	
10:30 a.m.		10:30 a.m.		10:30 a.m.		10:30 a.m.		10:30 a.m.		10:30 a.m.		10:30 a.m.	
11:00 a.m.		11:00 a.m.		11:00 a.m.		11:00 a.m.		11:00 a.m.		11:00 a.m.		11:00 a.m.	
11:30 a.m.		11:30 a.m.		11:30 a.m.		11:30 a.m.		11:30 a.m.		11:30 a.m.		11:30 a.m.	
12:00 p.m.		12:00 p.m.		12:00 p.m.		12:00 p.m.		12:00 p.m.		12:00 p.m.		12:00 p.m.	
12:30 p.m.		12:30 p.m.		12:30 p.m.		12:30 p.m.		12:30 p.m.		12:30 p.m.		12:30 p.m.	
1:00 p.m.		1:00 p.m.		1:00 p.m.		1:00 p.m.		1:00 p.m.		1:00 p.m.		1:00 p.m.	
1:30 p.m.		1:30 p.m.		1:30 p.m.		1:30 p.m.		1:30 p.m.		1:30 p.m.		1:30 p.m.	
2:30 p.m.		2:30 p.m.		2:30 p.m.		2:30 p.m.		2:30 p.m.		2:30 p.m.		2:30 p.m.	
3:00 p.m.		3:00 p.m.		3:00 p.m.		3:00 p.m.		3:00 p.m.		3:00 p.m.		3:00 p.m.	
3:30 p.m.		3:30 p.m.		3:30 p.m.		3:30 p.m.		3:30 p.m.		3:30 p.m.		3:30 p.m.	
4:00 p.m.		4:00 p.m.		4:00 p.m.		4:00 p.m.		4:00 p.m.		4:00 p.m.		4:00 p.m.	
4:30 p.m.		4:30 p.m.		4:30 p.m.		4:30 p.m.		4:30 p.m.		4:30 p.m.		4:30 p.m.	
5:00 p.m.		5:00 p.m.		5:00 p.m.		5:00 p.m.		5:00 p.m.		5:00 p.m.		5:00 p.m.	
5:30 p.m.		5:30 p.m.		5:30 p.m.		5:30 p.m.		5:30 p.m.		5:30 p.m.		5:30 p.m.	
6:00 p.m.		6:00 p.m.		6:00 p.m.		6:00 p.m.		6:00 p.m.		6:00 p.m.		6:00 p.m.	
6:30 p.m.		6:30 p.m.		6:30 p.m.		6:30 p.m.		6:30 p.m.		6:30 p.m.		6:30 p.m.	
7:00 p.m.		7:00 p.m.		7:00 p.m.		7:00 p.m.		7:00 p.m.		7:00 p.m.		7:00 p.m.	
7:30 p.m.		7:30 p.m.		7:30 p.m.		7:30 p.m.		7:30 p.m.		7:30 p.m.		7:30 p.m.	
8:00 p.m.		8:00 p.m.		8:00 p.m.		8:00 p.m.		8:00 p.m.		8:00 p.m.		8:00 p.m.	
8:30 p.m.		8:30 p.m.		8:30 p.m.		8:30 p.m.		8:30 p.m.		8:30 p.m.		8:30 p.m.	
9:00 p.m.		9:00 p.m.		9:00 p.m.		9:00 p.m.		9:00 p.m.		9:00 p.m.		9:00 p.m.	
9:30 p.m.		9:30 p.m.		9:30 p.m.		9:30 p.m.		9:30 p.m.		9:30 p.m.		9:30 p.m.	
10:00 p.m.		10:00 p.m.		10:00 p.m.		10:00 p.m.		10:00 p.m.		10:00 p.m.		10:00 p.m.	
10:30 p.m.		10:30 p.m.		10:30 p.m.		10:30 p.m.		10:30 p.m.		10:30 p.m.		10:30 p.m.	

Week Notes: _____

Weekly Tracker

New Leads

Contacts Found Through Referrals/Presentations/Marketing

Name:	**Rep** Cust
Phone:	
Email:	
Notes:	

Name:	**Rep** Cust
Phone:	
Email:	
Notes:	

Name:	**Rep** Cust
Phone:	
Email:	
Notes:	

Name:	**Rep** Cust
Phone:	
Email:	
Notes:	

Name:	**Rep** Cust
Phone:	
Email:	
Notes:	

Week Notes:

To Do List

Prioritize Top 3 Activities For The Day

Monday
☐
☐
☐

Tuesday
☐
☐
☐

Wednesday
☐
☐
☐

Thursday
☐
☐
☐

Friday
☐
☐
☐

Saturday
☐
☐
☐

Sunday
☐
☐
☐

Weekly Appointments

Month: _____   Year: _____

	Monday: ___	Tuesday: ___	Wednesday: ___	Thursday: ___	Friday: ___	Saturday: ___	Sunday: ___
	Appointments	Appointments	Appointments	Appointments	Appointments	Appointments	Appointments
8:00 a.m.							
8:30 a.m.							
9:00 a.m.							
9:30 a.m.							
10:00 a.m.							
10:30 a.m.							
11:00 a.m.							
11:30 a.m.							
12:00 p.m.							
12:30 p.m.							
1:00 p.m.							
1:30 p.m.							
2:30 p.m.							
3:00 p.m.							
3:30 p.m.							
4:00 p.m.							
4:30 p.m.							
5:00 p.m.							
5:30 p.m.							
6:00 p.m.							
6:30 p.m.							
7:00 p.m.							
7:30 p.m.							
8:00 p.m.							
8:30 p.m.							
9:00 p.m.							
9:30 p.m.							
10:00 p.m.							
10:30 p.m.							

Week Notes: _____

www.ingramcontent.com/pod-product-compliance
Lightning Source LLC
Chambersburg PA
CBHW041702200326
41518CB00002B/162